INSPIRED CHILDREN

INSPIRED CHILDREN

by

Olive M. Jones

INSPIRED CHILDREN
Copyright, 1933
Printed in the United States of America
Fifth Printing
B-I
ISBN 1-4392-6018-4

CONTENTS

—

Part Two

THE WAY. HOW CHILDREN LEARN TO KNOW GOD

INTRODUCTION

THIS book presents the first detailed description of the influence of the Oxford Group Movement (in America called A First Century Christian Fellowship) upon the lives of children. Some of us have been watching this influence with growing interest as year by year parents and teachers have come to a deeper experience of Christ, and found it altering their relations with children. It has come to be one of the most fascinating, and one of the most promising, of all the phases of the work of the Groups.

The author, Miss Olive M. Jones, is an educator of world-wide prominence. For more than twenty years she cared for the public schools in New York where the problem-children were taught, and in the field of behavior problems she stands second to none in both knowledge and experience. In 1923 she was made president of the National Education Association; she has been repeatedly a delegate to national and international conferences on education; her name is everywhere known in such circles.

But, as she tells in this book, when she came to us she could not have written a book of this kind. It would have been a technical treatise on religious education, pedagogically flawless, spiritually wanting. One of the extraordinary things that the Group Movement does is to deal with all people upon the basis of their own personal needs. Here was a great educator, a great public servant, a person who believed in religion, but without a vital personal religious experience herself. It seems to me that the danger of some religious education has been that it has assumed that anyone could be a teacher of religion who knew the facts of religion and the methods of teaching. But to this must be added the third requirement as most important of all—a personal religious experience. It was something over two years after the advent of Miss Jones to Calvary Church that we invited her to take over the church school and superintend it. During those two years she was growing up spiritually, after a true conversion, just as these children whom she describes are growing up now. If I may say so without impropriety, a tremendous thing has taken place when a person of such immense natural force, wide experience, and tremendous personal will gives herself to God, learns to live by His direction, and to merge her own life with that of a group of people who, in a company as at the first, are winning back for our generation what Dr. Jacks called "the lost radiance of the Christian religion." I have watched this experience from the first, and none is in a better position than I to witness to the fact of it, the power of its influence on others, and its growth year by year in further reaches of Christian consecration.

During the summer of 1928, just before we were entering Calvary House, our newly built parish house, there came guidance to me one day to ask Miss Jones to become director of the House and superintendent of the church school. I knew nothing of her finances; I only knew that ours would not permit of giving her a salary, and told her that I wanted her as a volunteer. She tucked the idea away in her mind, went off for a six weeks' vacation, and reported for duty on October 1st. Where God guides He provides; the way was made possible.

She took over a church school which, under my predecessor, had been quite well attended, but which, in the years when we had no parish house and when many of our people had moved away, had run down to about forty children a Sunday. I knew that the numerical problem was the least serious. The great problem was to get some religion into the school which would attract and transform the children. They used to have a formal assembly, sparsely attended; the classes were disorderly groups scattered about the body of the church; the children were noisy and inattentive. Today the assembly is reverent, gladly attended because the service is understood, and the discipline is practically perfect—this last a direct result of the religious experience of the children. There is an enrollment of 140, and an average attendance of about 100. The teachers, who had been ill-trained, and few of whom had had a personal experience of Christ, are now a well-equipped, consecrated group of persons, whose chief aim in their classes is not the imparting of information about religion, but the living out with the children of their own religious experience, helping these little ones to be then and there in touch with the living Christ, through study, through worship, above all through listening prayer and guidance. It has been our discovery that, far from this message being too advanced for children, they take to it like ducks to water.

Calvary Church is in a downtown neighborhood, with

relatively few families in near reach of us. We may never have a numerically large church school. What you find in this book is not sure to increase your numbers. What it will increase is the faith and spiritual conviction of your children. What else matters? I feel, and have felt from the first, that the Oxford Group Movement is simply the Church of Christ at work; and that all its discoveries and its power must be made available for the Church. It has been our privilege, in the school of Calvary Church, to see for the first time worked out systematically, and applied to a steady curriculum, the spirit of this Movement, which is only the spirit of early Christianity. The two great ingredients of this happy experiment have been a personal experience of Christ, and a knowledge of the science of teaching. These two factors had to be harmonized in the mind and heart of one creative and directive personality, before they could be anything but two diverse aims in actual practice, and this combination is found richly in the author of this book, without whom the experiment in Calvary Church School would probably never have been made.

But you will see that this book does not stop with the functions of a church school. It deals also with the relations between children and their parents in the home. Some of the most thrilling stories to which we have listened in house-parties, or at Thursday-night meetings at Calvary, have been those of parents who told us, often with much merriment, of the way their children's lives had been affected by the Groups, and of the way their own lives had been affected by the children. The family quiet time provides two indispensable things for the unity of a family: first, a creative part every day for the children in family worship; and second, a clearing-house for those feelings and plans, those misunderstandings and repressions, which tend to make for secrecy on the part of the children, and wall out the parents just when they are needed most. Some of the children told of in this book are already in their early adolescence; and the candor which obtains between them and their parents, with Christ as the center of their relationships, is a sure sign that these children will avoid the pain and inner isolation which spelled adolescence for so many in time past. Indeed, there are some of us who believe that the Oxford Group Movement, as it affects children, is doing nothing less than open to the world of parents a natural way in Christ by which their children may grow up without the fears and secrecies which were the breeding-ground for wrong-doing and for maladjustments of many kinds; but instead may be, from the very beginning, happy, mentally healthy, spiritually integrated personalities. I would caution you not to think that this can be brought about merely by atmosphere; children in the Groups, like all children, strike snags, and these have to be got over by spiritual decisions made in the same way as adults make them. The initial willingness to coöperate with Christ and one's parents is the beginning of the "conversion" of the child, often centering, as with grown-ups, in some crucial decision to take the right and guided way.

It is superfluous for me to commend this book. I

believe that it can and will be a life-saver to teachers and parents who now grope in darkness for a practical way to make Christ real to their children. I pray for it a wide and constant use. No one else known to me could have brought to the task of writing such a book the extraordinary combination of educational and religious experience which has been the life of the author. Most of the children written about are known to me personally. They are the happiest children whom I have ever known, and I could wish that there were a world full of them growing up to help mold the next era of human existence.

SAMUEL M. SHOEMAKER, JR.

Calvary Church
New York City

PART ONE

True Stories
of
Children's Spiritual Experience

CHAPTER I

"A LITTLE CHILD SHALL LEAD THEM"

THUS can be truly described my own coming into a personal religious experience and the reason for this book. But for a boy's question, challenging the honesty of my urging religious instruction upon him, I might still be included among the non-church-going, practically pagan, people. The release and peace, the discovery of the reality of God, and that inner certainty of faith which gives a reason for life—all these have been mine in these last six best years of my life. I might never have known them except that a child's challenge led me eventually into contact with the Oxford Groups, the First Century Christian Fellowship, as we often call it in America.

At the time, 1927, I was in charge of a group of schools for delinquent boys, including many types ranging from mere naughtiness to actual criminality. I had started this work twenty-one or two years earlier, believing that segregation in day schools under specially trained teachers with activities adjusted to their individual temperaments and aptitudes could reform boys without removing them from their normal environment, while at the same time an effort could be made to improve the particular condition which had precipitated their delinquency, results impossible to attain in the best of institutions. My educational theory then included ethical teaching, habit formation, and pre-vocational training, aided by medical and social service.

My faith in this theory was without limit at first. Difficulties and obstacles, whether financial, political, or personal, meant only a part of the game, a battle in which I must come off victor. From the point of view of service to the city school teachers, the work was one hundred per cent successful. As compared with social service, the percentage of success topped any of its claims. The prestige of the day school for truant and delinquent boys was great and even international.

But I was not satisfied. My own highest hopes were not being realized. It was the *whole* life of the boy I wanted to see set going on the straight road, not only the school-day period of his life, but his manhood. As the years passed on and the boys grew to manhood, my grief at the number of failures increased. A study of the after-school careers of the boys revealed seventy-nine per cent of them living useful, respectable lives, and this met with great acclaim. To me it meant twenty-one per cent of the boys on the road to prison, social menaces at best. To repair the lack, whatever it might be, campaigns for improved legislation became added to my plans—child-labor laws, child-welfare legislation, probation laws, the children's court, and many more. I rushed into the work for each one, and I still remember joyfully and gratefully my share in each of these campaigns for recognition of the rights of childhood.

A few years of outward-seeming success followed, accompanied by an almost unbearable sense of inward discouragement and defeat. Nominally a member of a Protestant church, actually I had no religious faith, and so many years had passed since I had given any more than an occasional attendance at any church that I never thought of it at all. I felt that the church had failed me in my time of greatest need and life-wrecking temptation. So I had discarded it. My university studies had weakened my faith in God, and I welcomed humanism as a creed by which I could live without secret longing for suicide or death in some form. I had found a Godless, churchless righteousness, I thought. Any connection between the work for children and for education in which I was so absorbingly interested and religion or even my own humanistic thinking never even occurred to me. Religion was my personal problem, nobody else's business, and the field of my thinking about it was carefully protected by signs to keep off the grass. I never spoke of it.

Still feeling keenly the defects in my educational theory, I began to think about religious education as a device to add to my list. That it might work for a few more of the boys was my only thought. Shortly before this, a movement for week-day religious education of unchurched children had started among New York City teachers, a voluntary activity, Roman Catholic and Protestant teachers working separately but in absolute harmony, in their leisure hours. The leaders in the Protestant organization asked me to help especially in securing publicity in which I had many years of experience. Mindful of my own plan to use it as a device for my boys, I accepted, never dreaming that God would use this act to bring me to Him.

In order to write publicity material, I had to see the work first hand and I visited some of the classes. One day, a small boy looked up into my face, as I looked at his exercises, and said, "What church do you go to?" His unconscious emphasis on *you* made me feel like a hypocrite, for I could not tell him none and I gave him an evasive answer, the church in which I had been confirmed. I had always tried hard to be honest with children, whatever I might do in other places or with grown-ups. Yet I had lied to that boy and on the subject of religion, which I felt most deeply in spite of my lack of faith.

Several days later, I decided to "save my face" with the children in the future by beginning to attend some church, preferably an Episcopal one, the denomination to which I belonged. Thinking about it in a street car one day, I looked up at the car cards carrying advertisements and read, "Calvary P. E. Church, Twenty-first Street and Fourth Avenue, Rev. Samuel M. Shoemaker, Jr., Rector. Come." I lived in a hotel on another corner of the same street myself, and on my return home I said to my friend who lived with me, "I'm going to this church on the corner next Sunday. The minister there must be an up-and-coming one. He has an ad in a street car. Some nerve for a clergyman." Not in many a long day had I even glanced at any item of religious news in any paper or journal. Therefore the name Shoemaker carried no significance to me, nor had I ever heard or read of Dr. Buchman, the Oxford

Group, the Fellowship, nor did I have any acquaintance associated with them to my knowledge. I went to church for several Sundays thereafter, greatly attracted by the practical sincerity of the sermons and by the cordiality of the people. That was in February of 1927.

In May of 1927 I wrote Mr. Shoemaker a letter, asking what steps I must take to become a member of his church if my long lapse from church attendance prevented a transfer. In the interview that followed he told me about the Thursday-night Group meeting. I listened, but mentally resolved not to go and not to be "pulled into" any church work. I was still only "saving my face" by a surface of honesty beneath which no one had a chance to see. Even though I did not know it, however, God's hand was in it all. He certainly guided Sam Shoemaker in the next step taken, for he asked a woman who knew me by reputation in women's organizations, herself a member of the Groups, to see me. She invited me to dine with her at a well-known woman's club, and over the dinner table she told me, simply and naturally, the story of the change Christ had wrought in her life. Struck by its reality and interpreting it in the light of the sermons I had been listening to, I knew I was seeing, hearing, truth in spiritual things at last. Then and there I made the first decision to find God I had ever really made in my life.

Out of that decision has grown the experience referred to in the first paragraph of this chapter. The story of the six years (it is now 1933) does not belong in this book. Suffice it to say that each difficult surrender of a sin has brought a new assurance of faith and a sense of release, of power, of spiritual and mental certainty, such as I never knew in my happiest days of pride and confidence in my own unbreakable will. Among its fruits have been intimate acquaintance and the privilege of being a trusted worker with Dr. Buchman in his world-wide campaign of winning souls for Jesus Christ, of helping to bring people, individually, into a natural and real experience of the things of the spirit.

Closest of all in relationship to this book was the call from Mr. Shoemaker to be superintendent of Calvary Church School and to begin the first experiment in religious education on the basis of the principles of Christ as taught and practiced by the Groups. The pages which follow are the outcome. The teachers in the school have been most devotedly interested and coöperative. Many parents of children far away from Calvary Church School have kept in close touch and have been equally coöperative. These two, parents and teachers of the Fellowship (the Oxford Group), have contributed much of the material, and I have often been only a compiler and a voice for them.

The stories which follow really happened. They prove the sensitiveness of children to spiritual things, and they indicate clearly the process by which that sensitiveness can be transmuted into life-controlling principle.

I have been four years collecting these stories of how children learn to know God and of the reality of their spiritual experience. My hope is that those who doubt that little children can grasp the principles fundamental to our approach to God will have their scepticism removed and that those who pass over lightly or negligently the tremendous truth that Jesus meant us to learn when he said, "Feed my lambs," will feel conviction for a sin greater than any the world calls sin.

CHAPTER II

Inspired Children

STORIES of actual occurrence of spiritual things in the lives of children will serve far better than wordy descriptions to make the issues of religious education clear. The writer can vouch for the essential truth of each of the following stories of children's discovery and understanding of principle. In many instances names or conditions have been changed slightly, in order not to reveal the actual identity of the child, for reasons which will be obvious to the reader.

"SHOULD HE FIGHT?"

Sinclair had never been to a city school. All his teaching had been given to him by mother or nurse and for a time in a small private school carrying only the very lowest grades. There was no private school for children of his age in the district where he lived, and he was too small and too delicate to go away to a boarding-school. Reluctantly, his parents decided to send him to the local school for a year or two, despite the unfavorable reputation of the discipline of the school.

But Sinclair had some playmates who had already begun to attend this school and they told large and terrible stories of fighting and of what the "big fellows"

would do to a "new guy." Visions of black eyes and of
bloody nose and of swollen face and of kicks and blows
haunted him every night, as each day brought him some
new detail of the fights ahead of him. Even his mother
became infected by his fears, especially as other parents
gave some confirmation of the stories Sinclair heard,
and she shared his anxiety about what he should do.

Brought up in a home where loud words were unknown, and taught to believe that war and all forms of
fighting were wicked and were done only because people
were selfish and let their tempers make them act like
animals, Sinclair faced a serious situation for a nine-
year-old boy. What was he to do? His mother, an earnest Christian and familiar with Fellowship principles,
suggested a quiet time to him, but it brought him no
release from his fears, nor to his mother herself. Realiz-
ing that her own attitude of fear for the boy and regret
that he must go to the dreaded school were barriers
between her and her reception of God's guidance, she
hesitated to continue quiet times with him lest his boyish
faith in prayer should suffer. She struggled to surrender the whole issue to God and to trust His wisdom
and His will, but her mother-love yielded with difficulty.

Then a woman friend in the Fellowship came to the
home to stay a few days. Sinclair and this friend had
been very chummy together at the time of previous
visits, so he told her his troubles and his fear, then concentrated particularly on the bloody nose. One of the
boys had told him that day about putting beefsteak on
the inevitable black eye when he got it, and his interest

in that experiment had temporarily overcome that promised horror. But there still remained a vision of streams of blood and the shame of being a "new guy."

The friend, being more familiar than the mother with boys' yarns and aware that there would probably be more threats and gesturing than actual fighting, suffered no fears about the boy's possible injuries, and she too suggested a quiet time. The boy and she both prayed and then waited in quiet. Suddenly the lad jumped up and ran off. The friend then heard of the previous, ineffective quiet time. Mother and friend consulted together about what to do, both by this time more concerned about the boy's faith than the threatening fights.

But at bedtime the little lad came bashfully into the friend's room and said: "You know I thought I'd better have a quiet time about that bloody nose all alone with God and so I did and He told me that it isn't the fight that matters but whether I'm a coward and so I won't be afraid any more." It was all just as breathlessly said as that unpunctuated sentence would indicate, and with a hasty kiss he ran away to bed. Nor has he been afraid, even though he did have to take his share of some crude and rough bullying when he went to school.

"I WON'T HAVE ANY MORE QUIET TIMES"

Peggy is blonde and rotund and full of life and energy. Her parents are among the "comfortable folks," although not rich enough to have many servants, and Peggy must do her share of little duties at home, both because her help is needed and because her mother wisely considers it necessary training. She is in the center of most things going on at our church school, is in all the plays, and gets many rewards for attendance and work.

Her teacher has been very successful in quiet times with her class and in leading them into a real understanding of spiritual things, even though her oldest pupil is only eleven. Peggy is not the oldest.

One Sunday morning, Peggy breezed in very noisily and continued to talk and move around after the quiet time began. Miss D. finally looked up and said, "Peggy, if you don't want to have a quiet time this morning, please be polite enough to let the rest of us listen to God." Peggy subsided, but she took no part in the quiet time.

Next Sunday morning, she went in late and announced as the reason that she had given up having quiet times and had arrived late in order to avoid the one in class. Miss D. realized that here was a real problem to meet and that Peggy's noise of the previous Sunday had a deeper significance than she had thought. As all the girls had heard all that had happened both Sundays, secret and individual settling of the difficulty would only precipitate new problems with the other girls. She laid aside her lesson-plan and said to Peggy: "Well, Peggy, I think we should all hear why you object to the quiet time. Do you think we all ought to give it up?"

Peggy replied: "It's this way, Miss D., when I have quiet time, God talks to me, and I don't want to hear

Him. You see, He tells me to do things I don't want to do and so I'm not going to listen or have quiet times any more."

Inquiry by teacher and other girls as to specific examples of what she meant brought forth the reply: "Well, you see, mamma tells me I must wash the dishes or else hold the baby while she does the dishes. I hate washing dishes and I don't want to hold the baby. I want to read. So I had a quiet time and I asked God to tell mamma to stop asking me to do the dishes. Instead, He told me I ought to do the dishes and I won't, and so I'm not going to have quiet time any more."

The teacher said a quick prayer for God to guide her with this child. Then aloud she said: "Girls, I don't know what to say to Peggy. Let us all ask God for guidance. Peggy, you may stay or not, as you choose." Needless to say she stayed, and an unusually long quiet time followed. The teacher prayed earnestly within her own mind, as the girls sat, some quiet, some writing, some praying, some even giggling.

Then the sharing began. Peggy herself said: "God told me to tell mamma I am sorry for being mean about the dishes and that it's no use not having a quiet time so as not to have to do things you don't want to do. If you ought to do them, God tells you, anyhow."

During a call made later at this same home, the mother exclaimed about the change in Peggy and said: "Is it the religion you teach at that school? How do you do it?"

Is there need to print a moral? Is it not clear that this child grasped the ideas of surrender, confession, restitution, and guidance, and applied them to the unwelcome task of washing the dishes? Is it any harder for you to apply them to your relationships in your home? May not learning them in the duty of washing the dishes prepare her to apply them in succeeding and equally unwelcome duties? May it not establish in her the habit of obeying God's guidance?

A LITTLE ANGEL?

Ruth seemed to be a little saint. She was apparently sweet-tempered and unselfish, ready to help in class, popular with the other girls, beloved by the teacher, and often lovingly accosted by the superintendent of the church school. She came to class regularly and always shared in the quiet time. She talked, naturally and without any self-consciousness or boasting spirit, about her quiet times at home. Once she shared that God had told her she ought to have midday prayers.

The teachers thought she had no problems. It seemed as if their only duty was to fix firmly her faith and her reliance on God so that later conditions in life could not shake them. At ten years old she was a "budding angel," as one teacher described her.

Then came a quiet time one Sunday morning, and Ruth's sharing was tearfully told. She said that God had told her not to stamp her foot at her mother when she was asked to do the ironing. It was evident to the teacher that there was conviction of sin, but only unwilling repentance and no real intention of making confession to mother or of changing. Here was no saint, but a human child with real problems! The teacher learned that not even "budding angels" could escape them.

Prayer was the only way to find the answer. Not only Ruth and the teacher, but all the girls in the class prayed for God to help her. Unaided by word of teacher or mother, the child's own guidance from God taught her to apologize to mother, to overcome her temper, and to be helpful at home, where no one, it was learned later, had any delusion that she was either saint or budding angel, but where all also remarked on her new and helpful conduct. A teacher, in commenting on this incident, said: "My first impulse, when I heard of Ruth's outbreak, was to reproach the mother for over-working a small child, but God has higher standards of behavior for children than I, and He has His own way of guiding them into truth."

HER TIRESOME LITTLE BROTHER

Nellie, aged ten, had a small brother for whom she was often responsible. She used this responsibility as an opportunity to exercise a somewhat dictatorial temperament. She "bossed" him in their play in the home and on the street, so that conflicts were frequent and angry. He was slower mentally than she and often could not do his lessons. To Nellie this was another chance, and she laughed at him, teased him, and shamed him.

These things were unknown to the teacher whose class Nellie had joined late in the year. Other girls explained to Nellie what a quiet time is, why they held it, and related some of their own experiences. The teacher waited to make sure that Nellie understood and was really praying and sincerely "listening" for guidance. Then one day, before the quiet time began, the teacher said: "Nellie, do you think God will speak to you now? Will you join in our class quiet time today?"

The child's reply assured the teacher that Nellie was really ready and that neither imitative nor dishonest sharing need be guarded against. After the prayer was made, Nellie joined in the sharing which followed, saying: "God says I must stop laughing at Bunny when he can't do his lessons, but I must help him and not boss him."

The trouble in the home ended, not all at once, of course, for who expects old heads on young shoulders? But improvement began at once. And this is worthy of note—in later quiet-time sharing, Nellie herself provided the opportunity for follow-up work by the teacher in order to see that the change was not a spasmodic thing, but genuine and continuing.

CONFESS YOUR OWN SINS

Margaret and Maude were companions in the same class, a group of girls ranging from ten to twelve years of age. All through the year they had shared in the class quiet times and joined with the teacher in prayer and in Bible study.

One day the Scripture reading was the thirteenth chapter of First Corinthians. The teacher read aloud from Moffatt's translation. She paused after reading

"Love makes no parade," and said, "Do we ever show off?" Margaret spoke up quickly, exclaiming, "Yes, Maudie does."

Maude protested, but no comment was made by the teacher, and the quiet time soon followed. Margaret's turn to share came. She read from her notebook much the same as she usually did, and then she said: "But here at the end it says, 'Don't judge.' I wonder why. I don't judge." There was a silence. The other girls sat still, waiting for the teacher to speak. The teacher had learned to wait for God to guide in all such problems, and she sat praying that His Holy Spirit might open Margaret's mind to understand the message received in quiet time. Finally Margaret looked up and said: "Why, yes, I do judge. I judged Maudie just now. I'm sorry."

Can any one doubt the reality of this child's approach to God or of her comprehension of the conditions by which we come to Him?

A BOYISH LARK?

During one summer Martin Scott helped out in a Daily Vacation Bible School in a section known as Milltown. He had under his care a large group of boys ranging in age from twelve to sixteen. They were pretty tough. They had no religious education outside of the little, and that exceedingly formal, Bible instruction of occasional itinerant evangelists.

To make God a friend and not a dreaded Being somewhere far away, to make Jesus Christ known as the Son sent by a loving God instead of a name and word mentioned only in cursing and swearing, these were the aims for which Martin labored and prayed all summer. Prayer, the quiet time, God's voice in guidance, these were the means, under God, he sought to use and to teach the boys to know.

I have heard teachers, themselves living Christian lives and teaching principle as voiced by the Fellowship, speak sceptically of the possibility of making boys of the age and type of Martin's boys willing to join in a quiet time or able to get anything out of it, especially in group sharing. I have seen teachers fail and even lose a class as they tried, honestly tried, to lead their boys to pray and to listen for guidance. I have seen them give it up and come to me, saying: "These older boys cannot be reached by group quiet times. I'll only lose them, for they won't come. I must depend on individual handling, individual talks." Therefore Martin's efforts during the summer were of especial interest to me. His results prove that somewhere, somehow, these other teachers failed in faith or in love or in boy-knowledge. The story of how a miscalled boyish lark was straightened out is illustrative of Martin's solution of the problem.

He took some fourteen of these boys on a camping trip. The camp was built on the property of a farmer who rented part of his land to an old man to raise watermelons. Fun and song and all the usual accompaniments of a well-conducted camping party made the trip a great success, Martin being experienced in Boy Scout work. For all he saw or heard, the boys had all been models of good behavior. But the next day he met the old farmer and learned from him that the boys had cut three of his watermelons and eaten them. Here was a discouraging problem for Martin.

The next school day he talked to all the boys about the old man and his loss, but he made no other comment, asked for no confessions, did no scolding or preaching. Later the quiet time came, and during the sharing the boys who had taken the watermelons and the boys who had eaten them confessed of their own free will. A quiet time with these boys followed some discussion of their act, among themselves, as to what they ought to do and whether they were to blame when they did not "mean" any harm. During the quiet time it came to all of them that they ought to go to the old man, confess and apologize, and also pay for the watermelons. There was no dissenting voice and not one who had not heard the same direction from God.

Nor did the story end there. They confessed, under guidance, that they had taken some cantaloupes from another farmer on another occasion and that they should restore for these, too. To some it meant asking their parents for the money, with probable anger and punishment at home as a consequence. Yet they agreed that they were obliged to confess to their parents as well.

Martin stood by and let them work it out for themselves. Not once did he suggest action. Not once did he use any influence upon them, except to advise quiet time and listening for guidance when they were in doubt or afraid. He went with them to the farmers and they made clean-cut confessions of their deed. They were much relieved when it was over, much ashamed, but satisfied that they had learned to see it as God saw it, that what seemed only a boyish lark was called dishonesty by God.

The incident had a wide-spreading influence among the boys; quiet time and sharing are not failures or unpopular there. The thrill of confession, restoration, and forgiveness for sin has been known.

DIRTY OVERALLS

Paul was an orphan in a community where misfortune brings as much scorn and hardship as sin, often more if the sinner is clever at concealing his guilt. Being an orphan, he was nobody's responsibility as to education, church, or home, and must earn by the sweat of his boyish brow the food given him and must content himself with cast-off clothes, often bestowed only after dirt and holes had made his condition shocking to the consciences of even his townspeople. He was not a happy boy and therefore not a very good one. Yet he had native gifts of fun-making which brought him companionship among boys not so fastidious as their elders about his offense of being an orphan and a financial liability.

The boys in his little town decided to give an ice-cream party to raise money for their ball team. They appointed committees to arrange plans and prices, people to be invited, and the serving of the ice-cream. This last-named committee argued hotly, pro and con, regarding the appearance of the ice-cream servers as over against the probable soiling of best clothes in the process of serving. Then one boy, very influential in the group, broke out: "If Paul serves, I'm not coming. He is sure to come in those dirty, smelly overalls and spoil the looks of things." Consternation prevailed. Paul's witty quips as he served would make sales, but what about those overalls?

The teacher, the same one as in the story, "A Boyish Lark," suggested that before any more hasty remarks were made, they pray about it and let God make the decision about Paul. At the close of the quiet time the boys saw things quite differently. Instead of not wanting Paul, they decided they wanted him clean and dressed like the others.

How was it to be done? It meant the purchase of white trousers and a shirt. Spend money for clothes for Paul when they had to raise money to run their ball team? Absurd. And people knew Paul had no money to buy white trousers; they would think he stole them. And how did you know but Paul would get mad at their talking about his clothes? Didn't he always "make out" he didn't care about his overalls, but would go where he wanted to, anyhow, whether people liked his overalls or not? More quiet time and then the rapid rush of ideas about how it could all be done.

"We will all chip in," was the unanimous voice. "We'll say nothing to Paul nor to any of the other boys. Let the teacher take care of seeing that Paul receives the new clothes and that people know he got 'em honestly." And so it was done. A proud and happy server was Paul, and the lesson in practical love gained by the boys on the team was worth more than any sermon.

This happened early in the summer. The new clothes

and the knowledge that his boy companions wanted him enough to sacrifice for him made a different boy of Paul. Best of all, the boys have learned that God guides in the details of life, as well as in making us conscious of sin, and that His way of settling a difficulty is better than human argument.

BILLY'S FAITH

Billy was twelve and his sister Betty was nine. Billy was tremendously fond of his sister, watched over her, and only unwillingly separated from her. One summer, they were both in the same class in Daily Vacation Bible School.

The teacher noticed, during the morning exercises, one day, that Billy was paying no attention to her or to the class, but kept looking out of the window with a troubled look on his face. The teacher questioned him. He said he was worried about his sister, that she had started out to school with him but had turned back for something, telling him not to wait or he would be late. She had not arrived at the school. Poor Billy was genuinely anxious. He felt responsible for Betty, blamed himself for not waiting for her, and wanted to go and look for her. The teacher asked him to wait until the quiet time was over, promising that if she had not come in, he might go to look for her then.

When the quiet time ended, Billy's face was radiant. "God told me not to worry about Betty," he exclaimed, when he shared his quiet time guidance; "she didn't feel well and stayed home after she got there." Such later proved to be the case. But Billy needed no confirmation of his guidance or of his faith. He worked happily and contentedly all the morning, and at noon went home to "see if Betty is better." He believed God when he heard His voice.

THORNS

During Lent one year our church school had weekday sessions as a special Lenten service. The time was spent in study of the parables of Christ. A class of twelve-year-old girls was at work on the parable, "The Sower and the Seed," when the following incident occurred.

The class read, "Some fell upon thorny ground and the thorns sprang up and choked it." They paused and discussed this passage. City children do not always know what thorns are, and the metaphor had to be made clear. They talked about what might have been the "thorns" Jesus had in His mind. They talked about the "thorns" people find in the way today.

By general agreement then they had a class quiet time, praying God to tell them what were the "thorns" that kept them from being "good ground." Sharing followed. Remember that the sharing is never, must never be, compulsory, but a free act to be done or not, as guided.

One girl said that the thorn in her life was fear of the dark. She told how far-reaching were the consequences of this fear. It kept her from going to bed on time because she would not go upstairs alone. That made her sleepy in school and her marks suffered. She told the class that she would go to bed on time that night, even if she were afraid, and she would ask God to take away her fear. She did as she said. The fear of the dark has never returned!

In later quiet times she told how that victory had helped her to gain victory over other fears as they came along. Her marks in school improved rapidly and her conduct changed from dull silence to normal, laughing girlhood. The power of Christ, not the special tests and treatment of psychoanalysts, "woke up" this mind. The guidance of God in quiet time removed the obstructing fear.

LEARNING VERSUS OBEYING

A child of eight joined our church school a couple of years ago. She had learned many Bible verses by heart, including the Ten Commandments, and could reel them off like a phonograph record. She knew most of the stories the class she entered was learning.

But she had acquired none of the attitudes of gentleness or unselfishness or politeness which the stories were supposed to teach. She liked to "show off" her recitation of Bible verses and she was scornful of the stories as "old stuff," although she could answer no questions as to what the stories meant. She always took the best seat, claimed the forefront of attention all the time, and constantly interrupted the person speaking with demands for attention to her needs and inquiries. The other children disliked her heartily.

It was very difficult to teach her to pray or to join with any sincerity or reality in class quiet times. For a year, the teacher saw no encouraging signs of change. But a year later, in a class where all the children kept regular quiet times, they were all learning the Ten Commandments, already familiar to her. A quiet time followed the lesson one day. When the chance for sharing came to her, she entered into it, honestly, for the first time, and said: "God told me to learn and obey the Ten Commandments," her emphasis on the words, "and obey," showing clearly that she understood the full significance.

Sometimes we too have learned *words*, without spirit, and are even slower than Mabel in seeing the difference.

THE RUMBLE SEAT

Can you imagine how wonderful it is to be a twelve-year-old girl who has a teacher that drives her own car and it has a rumble seat? Especially when she occasionally takes out for a ride as many girls as can be packed into the car!

One day a group of twelve-year-old girls were having a quiet time with their teacher. She had been talking to them about going for a ride after the lesson. So their thoughts turned in anticipation of the ride even during the quiet time. One little girl shared that she had "guidance" to ride in the rumble seat.

It seemed to the teacher to be more the voice of the child's desire than the voice of God. She recognized the opportunity to teach some of the principles of guidance and said: "I wonder if God really told you to ride in the rumble seat? You see, there are ways of finding out if what comes to you is really guidance. Shall we talk about them a while?"

The children agreed and seemed to understand and truly desire to know. Maybe some of them had been puzzled and troubled about deciding whether human wish or God's guidance controlled the promptings of the quiet time. The teacher began:

"We have tests by which we can decide between our wants and wishes and God's guidance. If what comes to you breaks one of these tests, it is not God's guidance. The first is the test of absolute honesty. For instance, God would never tell you to take apples from Farmer Harden's trees." (The class was in a country school.)

The children nodded their heads in agreement and the teacher continued with the second test, that of absolute love. She told them that God would never tell them to go off to play and leave the baby or to slap their younger brothers and sisters. Again they understood. Encouraged, the teacher came to the third test, which would really apply to her problem of the rumble seat, and she said, not too seriously:

"The third way of testing guidance is to be sure it is absolutely unselfish. Now God might tell you to ride in the rumble seat if it were a rainy day and the car were crowded. Then it would be unselfish to offer to ride in the rumble seat. But on a clear day do you think it is unselfish? God might tell me which girls to put there today, but I do not think He would tell the girls themselves."

That was the end of selfish requests in the name of guidance. Some one would always say, "Rumble seat!"

BILLY'S GUIDANCE

Billy is nine years old and lives in Kentucky. One time a man who believed in quiet time, who believed also in boys, and who, moreover, believed boys could and would have quiet times and hear God's guiding directions, visited Billy's home. He and Billy became great chums and had quiet times together.

One day, Billy wrote down his guidance as it came to him during the quiet time and gave it to this new, wonderful man friend of his. This man gave permission to print it in this series of stories aimed to show how genuine and real is the child's spiritual life when it is helped, not checked, by adult interference. The words in parentheses are words Billy could not spell and printed in afterwards from dictation. The page as he wrote it follows:

"I think I should be more honest and tell the truth. I think I should help mother with sister. I want you to help me not to steal and help Tom too. Help Dad and I to measure the pane. Last night I got mad at Tom help me not to get mad so quick. This morning I got mad too. Help me at school. Today help me to mind mother today at home help me not to be so (stingy) to be more happy and (courteous)."

SHE PEEKED INTO IT

Self-consciousness is a serious barrier to guidance. God cannot get through when we hinder Him by thinking of ourselves and of what others think of us. Hence, the sacred privacy which must be given to a child about his "guidance notebook," if he keeps one. He should be encouraged to share what comes, but no one should ever read it or tell it without his permission. The consequences to a child's spiritual life are tragic when parent or teacher violates this privacy.

Two teachers in our church school have had great difficulty with one little girl because her rights were not respected. She had kept her quiet times faithfully for at least two years, when suddenly she stopped. Even in class quiet time she reported that she had no guidance. Bessie was then about ten years old. The teachers believed that the trouble had arisen in the home and called on the mother.

The mother told of her amusement (!) over the child's quiet times. She told how greatly intrigued she had been by Bessie's guidance book. Finally she admitted that she had peeked into it when Bessie was not around. Of course, Bessie had discovered it, self-consciousness arose, and a barrier between the child and God.

The teachers realized that their immediate field of work was in that home. It is as yet an unfinished story, but Bessie at least again shares naturally in quiet times with her class and her teachers.

HIS GRADUATION PRAYER

It is a favorite theory that the adolescent boy is so hampered by the physical changes of his age that he is too self-conscious for it to be wise to press spiritual things upon him, lest he become introspective. My belief is that it is just the time in his life when understanding, sympathetic instruction concerning the spiritual life is most essential to prevent unhealthy introspection, to give balance to his thinking and a protection against the kind of reading and thinking he is all too apt to have thrust upon him then. Maybe he won't talk much and maybe he gropes dumbly for expression, but every once in a while we get a chance to see how deeply his spiritual life is being reached.

Charles' mother had such a chance recently. He had just been graduated from elementary school with highest honors, many prizes, and much commendation as the most "reliable" boy in his class. When it was over and he had returned home alone with his mother, he said, shyly and with face illumined by an inner light, "You know, mother dear, I would never have been so honored if I had not prayed so hard before graduation. I asked God to make you proud of me, and He answered my prayers."

THE BUN STORY

The bun story, as we have come to call it, has been told and printed so many times that at first I hesitated to include it here. But not only is it an absolutely true story, having happened in our church school, but it is so marvelously illustrative of principle and of children's understanding and willing obedience to principle that I cannot leave it out.

It was a class of girls, exceedingly fortunate in having a teacher who had taught them to talk with God naturally and freely. Every lesson began with a prayer for God to guide the teaching and with a quiet time to "listen" for His direction, both personally and for the lesson.

One Sunday, while all were silently praying, with heads bowed, one little girl, seven years old then, prayed aloud, "God, forgive me for taking the bun." (Note as principle here: The voice of God speaks in the quiet time when we have all barriers down with the same simplicity as this child.) Nothing more was said by anyone then, and in the sharing time she said nothing further in explanation. After the lesson the teacher detained her and asked her privately what she meant. Then the story came out.

On the previous Friday her mother sent her to the bakery to buy a loaf of bread. A fresh batch of delicious cinnamon buns lay on the counter. She was tempted. The baker turned his back to wrap up the loaf of bread. No one was looking, so she took one and on the way home she ate it. The baker knew nothing about it. (Note as principle here: Temptation. Knowledge of wrong in that she would not have taken it if the baker had been looking. The sin not discovered.)

On Sunday in class, as she listened in the quiet time,

God told her it was wrong to steal and that taking the bun was stealing. The child was genuinely sorry and prayed for forgiveness. (Note: Conviction of sin. Repentance. Prayer for pardon.)

The teacher might have comforted the child and let the matter drop here, but her own experience of Christian living was real and deep. She knew there was another step—restitution. She asked the child, "Do you think God has forgiven you?" The little one hesitated and said, "I don't know." The teacher then suggested another quiet time to ask God if He really had forgiven her or whether there was something He wanted her to do.

A few seconds later, the child looked up and said: "I ought to take the bun back, but I can't, because I ate it up." Another silence, and then with a joyful smile she said: "I have three cents in my bank. I'll take that to the baker and pay him for the bun." Next day, together the teacher and child went to the baker and paid for the bun. (Note: The way of restitution shown. Surrender to God in acceptance of His way and the sacrifice it entailed. The joy of release and assurance of pardon for sin.)

DAVID

David was fortunate in his home. His father was a physician and his mother was most understanding in her loving training of David and his brother. Yet she felt that somehow she never quite reached the real David. She was conscious of something withheld, some depth of feeling, some hidden thinking which he never let her penetrate. Aware of the sad possibilities which may develop in a boy's unrevealed thinking, she conferred with J., a young man worker in the Groups then holding meetings in the town. J. and David became great chums and had many talks together. Finally came a quiet time, following some exchange of views about honesty. In the sharing time, J. told the boy about an experience of his own when he "cribbed" an examination in school. David looked up and said: "You mean to say you've cribbed? Why, I copy, too."

Asked what he ought to do about it, he had a quiet time and said his guidance was, "If I copy a lot, I must tell my teacher." He did not seem satisfied, however, and so J. suggested another quiet time. This time his guidance read, "If I copy any more, I must tell my teacher." J. inquired whether he had anything else to tell. After a third quiet time, David, this time without writing, looked up and said with a sigh of relief, "God tells me I must tell her about all the times I did it before." Then after a moment's reflection, he smiled and said, "I suppose I must tell all six of them." He had six teachers.

The whole gospel of conviction of sin, repentance, confession, and restitution had been truly learned in that quiet time with God the Guide and Teacher. His mother found him later to be still the cherub-faced, happy boy, but no longer the enigma he had been to her. In their sharing together, mutual trust and confidence have been greatly deepened and increased.

MEAD TELLS SKIPPY ABOUT THE DEVIL

Several stories of Mead will appear in this book, but I must tell one that has just come to me by mail as I write this chapter. Not so much because it illustrates any principle or method of discipline or religious education as because it proves the immediate personal application to their own lives children naturally make of religious truth they learn. Why do we break down that faith?

Mead's mother was trying to make him understand that he could choose to be good rather than to be naughty. She explained to him by sharing incidents in her own life, which he could understand or knew, how she had always the chance for a choice between right and wrong. In illustration, also, she told him the story of the Temptation in the Wilderness, how Jesus refused to do any of the wrong things the devil wanted him to do. She gave no description of the devil or statement about who he is. Mead was much impressed by the story, and by the idea that he was a "big boy" and could "*choose* to be good like Jesus did."

Some weeks passed and Mead joined his cousins at the grandmother's summer home. Mead is all of six months older than Skippy, his four-and-a-half-year-old cousin, and much, much older than Anne and Sterry, aged three and two, respectively! In spite of Mead's maturity, two governesses are needed to keep this lively quartet, not only well and happy, but safe. So they are absolutely forbidden to go to the beach or into the water unless some adult is with them.

The other day, Mead ran into the living-room and said to his grandmother, Mother T., as she is affectionately known to the Group:

"Nana, Skippy splashed me!"

"Splashed you? How do you mean?"

"Yes, he splashed me, when we went in wading."

"Why, Mead, I'm surprised at you. You know perfectly well, all of you, that you must never go to the beach without an older person."

"They didn't go alone, Nana. There was an older person. *I* was with them."

Here was a difficult situation for Nana, let alone that issue of choice between right and wrong. However, Mead found his own solution, as the sequel showed, when, a few days later, Madi, the governess, was giving the children their supper.

Said Mead, "Skippy, you know we were little devils when we went in the water."

An astonished Skippy, who had never known the devil by name before, replied, "Devils, what's that?"

Mead explained: "The devil is a kind of angel that doesn't help us to be good. Jesus was nearly made bad by the devil one day, when he was on earth. But now he is in heaven, so he is all right." Then, turning to Madi, "You will go there some day and you will see."

CHAPTER III

The Challenge of a Child's Faith

THE effect of the spontaneous response of children to real spiritual influences has been tremendous and has spread far more widely than can ever be measured.

One mother, previously indifferent to prayer and to church connections, found God through the lessons of her little girl's quiet times, as these quiet times were practiced by the child at home, following out voluntarily the idea of the quiet time learned in her class. One mother asked the church visitor to teach her what her children meant by talking about the quiet time, and for the first time there are family prayers in that home. A new teacher took over a class of boys. He failed to have the quiet time at the close of the lesson. A boy checked him, saying, "Why don't you ask God to bless the lesson you have taught us?"

A seven-year-old child, who was just learning about quiet times and was much thrilled by her experience, said, thoughtfully, to her mother one day: "Mother, Mrs. S. [her teacher] knows more about God than you do, and Mr. S. [the minister] knows more about Him than Mrs. S. because he went to school to learn about God." Many mothers may find themselves in such a position unless their own religious experience is as strong as their children's. This same child related all her discoveries to the maid who took her to Sunday school with such enthusiasm that the maids disputed about which should take her each week. They attended the service as a result and often went to the adult Bible class.

A mother, who had heard something about the work of the Fellowship and was interested herself, sent her six-year-old daughter to our church school. Here she learned enough about guidance and prayer to suggest a quiet time when her mother found one day that she had been dishonest. The mother had tried every other means of correction for her daughter's taking money to buy candy, but had been unsuccessful. So they had a quiet time and prayed. The child was never tempted again. Her mother was so much impressed that she came and talked to one of the staff of the church and found an experience of Christ for herself.

A principal of a school, herself sometimes the victim of violent rages, was once called upon to punish a boy who had been guilty of bad language and of striking the teacher during a fit of temper. In order to quiet the boy and also give him something to reflect upon, the principal told him to copy Proverbs 16:32 ("He that ruleth his spirit is greater than he that taketh a city"). The boy obeyed, then looked up at the principal and said, "Do you rule your spirit?" The words sank deeply home into that principal's heart. Although she had then neither knowledge of nor connection with the Fellowship, she and the boy "shared" their problems of temper together and agreed that since God had inspired the proverb, He would also help them both to "rule their spirit." The boy is dead, killed in action in 1917, during the World War, but the principal has since found Christ and victory over temper through the Fellowship and the message of guidance and sharing.

Mead's grandfather, his mother's father, died not long ago. Virginia had promised to take Mead to town, when the telephone called her to her father's bedside. She had to explain to Mead why she could not take him. She went into Mead's room, crying, and said:

"Mead, Pop is going away from us."

"Where is he going?"

"He is going to be with Jesus."

"Where?"

"In heaven."

"What are you crying for?"

"Well, I know it's selfish, but I don't want him to go away where I can't see him any more."

With his arms around her in comfort, said Mead: "You silly thing. You will see him when you get there!"

A chain of people steadily growing has found a vital experience of Christ through the influence of Prue, a nine-year-old child who learned to have a quiet time with her aunt while her parents were in Europe. After their return, the mother and then the father and since then a steadily increasing number of people, including some dignitaries of the church, have found Christ as a vitalizing experience and a living, daily guide for their actions. Truly a little child shall lead them!

Prue and Buddy, her brother, are links in a chain of

surrendered lives which has stretched across three continents. The story of their beginning, of the repeated challenge of their faith to their parents, follows, given almost verbatim as their mother wrote it to me.

It is quite natural for a child to think of God and to talk to Him. So with little Prue, who was nine years old, the only thing necessary was a person who knew our Heavenly Father as a reality in her own life to be able to make Him real to her. This was her aunt, who told her that she believed God had a plan for the world, that each one had a share in that plan, and that the way to find out one's part was through two-way prayer. She explained that she should talk to God first and then sit quietly and let Him talk to her. She said, "You won't hear a voice like Daddy's or Mummy's, but God will guide your own thoughts." So, quite naturally, Prue started keeping her quiet time each morning. In fact, at no one's suggestion, she appeared one day with a little notebook and announced that she was going to listen to God, too.

The mother was in Europe at the time and on her return she was delighted to find the child had found a religious experience. Always wanting religion for her children, she had never known quite what to do about it. She read them the Bible one whole winter at bedtime and heard their prayers. But she found that you cannot give away an experience you have not had yourself.

The mother, also named Prue, tried to talk to little Prue. This was before her own life was changed. Little Prue asked her mother what she thought about guidance. After some reflection she answered, "Why, I think it is your conscience telling you what to do." The child sat silent and thought for a moment, and then said, "No, Mummy, I don't believe it is; your conscience tells you the difference between right and wrong, but there might be six right things you could do, and guidance tells you which one God wants you to do."

"I knew then that to share in my child's spiritual life I would have to make a start myself," is the mother's comment on this incident.

Buddy is a year and a half younger than little Prue, and when he was nine went with their parents to their first house party. Buddy had gone to Prue that first winter to ask her to tell him how he could keep a quiet time, and he too had started listening to God. But he wasn't very serious about it until he came to that house party. There he was impressed, in the united quiet times, at seeing other people besides his own family listening to God. And one morning he stood up and shared the guidance that had come to him. It was real. The next day he shared that it had come to him in his early quiet time with his sister: "Don't laugh at other people; you are just as funny as they are yourself."

Later the parents talked with Buddy. He told them that he had always known that if he did certain things and got caught, he would be punished and that this was called "wrong"; also that certain other things he did were called "right." But his guidance was that he himself had the power to choose the right thing or the wrong thing. It had never occurred to him before that there was a choice for him.

The husband, George, tells an interesting story about himself. At the time he was very young spiritually; in fact his own experience had come only a few months before. "Big Prue" was ill one evening and asked him to say prayers with the children. So he knelt down between them, and as he was uncertain about proceedings he waited to follow the children's lead. First one prayed and then the other. George says he was all choked up over the simple reality of their talking to God. It cut into another area in him which had so recently been pagan. Then came a pause. Nothing happened. He waited in anxious silence. There came a nudge on one side, then a nudge on the other. Finally came a whisper, "Daddy, aren't you going to pray, too?" He prayed aloud for the first time, really shamed into it by the example of his own children's faith.

The following summer Buddy went away to camp. Father and Mother realized they would have to trust him entirely to God insofar as his spiritual life was concerned, that he would have no encouragement where he was going. At the end of three weeks they visited him, and the first thing he asked was, "Can we have a quiet time together?" When he went home, they learned he had kept his quiet time every single day but one the whole two months. Also his example had created such interest that his tentmates had joined him, and theirs was the only tent in camp where they all knelt down in prayer each night.

The summer after this, little Freddy, aged five, went away to camp. The woman who was in charge wrote, after he had been there two weeks, to know something more about the religious movement she had heard the family were a part of. His councilor had spoken to her about Freddy's prayers, and so he was asked if he would pray aloud at the church service on Sunday. He said he would if he didn't have to stand up in front. The natural simplicity of his prayer impressed the whole camp.

The next winter was a very difficult one for Bud. There was a change of schools and one of his masters was known for his disagreeableness. Then he took a dislike to Bud. The family talked it over at home and prayed about it. The parents offered him the opportunity to go elsewhere, but he refused. He said he wanted to stick it out. Each morning his guidance would be about his work, but it seemed as if, no matter how hard he tried, he would get no credit. His guidance was what to study in his study periods, what work to bring home, and what he needed more time on. Finally his reports began to improve and at the end of the year, through Buddy's guided effort, he had won the master's liking.

During this same winter Prue was going through the difficult age of adolescence. A famous child's specialist said once that adolescence is the time when your children are neither fish nor fowl; they are no longer children and not yet grown. They are very difficult to understand because they don't understand themselves. But if a mother wins her daughter's confidence at the beginning, she need no longer fear for her later on. I can think of no better way than to be on a sharing basis of fellowship at this time.

Prue skipped into her mother's room, one night, and told how she had been leading a Dr. Jekyll and Mr. Hyde life. At home, where influences were Christian, she lived according to God's will. In school, under worldly influences, she forgot what God wanted her to do and was all out for herself. She wanted to be popular, and she was, by outdoing everybody else. But she said she was miserable; she hated leading a double life and she wanted to live God's will all the time. So on her knees, very simply, she surrendered her will to God and asked Him to guide her moment by moment. Now she is thinking in terms of bringing God into the lives of her friends and the popularity she sought is now hers without seeking.

"Out of such experiences as these it is natural that it is our family habit to take our problems to God and He guides us through." Thus do these parents sum up the story of Prue and Buddy.

CHAPTER IV

CHILDREN'S "NATURAL" FAULTS

I HAVE debated on both sides of the doctrine of original sin. It used to be one of my favorite and often telling arguments that the doctrine of original sin was in itself a denial of God's power over the devil or an unconscious acknowledgment by religionists that there is neither God nor devil. I then joyfully welcomed the psychology of the behavioristic school, because it helped out my theory that we would all be "good children" if people and circumstances did not produce evil thinking and evil doing.

That was all before my intimate acquaintance with some homes where prayer brings the daily guidance and where the parents are living surrendered lives, truly seeking to make Christ the center of their training for their children. I shall not attempt here to give either psychological or doctrinal explanation of what I have seen and been told, but I assure you I never argue in the negative any more about the doctrine of original sin.

QUARRELING

The most conclusive evidence is in children's quarrels, even in homes where there is absolutely no example of discord. It is in these very instances of children's quarrels, however, that there have come the most striking evidences of the power of God through prayer and of the truth and reality of guidance from God coming through the "listening" of the quiet time.

One mother tells of her two children, a boy and a girl. She is herself using every effort, every means, to teach her children self-control, her own example being a great factor in her teaching. But the two children, although devoted to each other, occasionally have very serious quarrels. One morning they had a "regular pitched battle," as the mother describes it. Her impulse was to interfere, reason with them both, and, if necessary, punish. But it came to her to let them fight it out and wait for the quiet time.

Even then she said not a word about what had happened. They all prayed and then they were quiet, "listening," a phrase the children have given us about waiting for guidance, but which I use myself because it is so expressive. Anne, the little girl and much younger than Charles, the boy, was very serious as mother and two children meditated.

It came her turn to share guidance. "God told me," she said, "that Charles and I must be nice to each other, and that I must tell him I'm sorry." The mother's comment is, "For days after that incident there was peace in our little home." The comment tells that neither child was any more a "budding angel" than Ruth of an earlier story, but it does show the *way* to bring peace through the conviction of wrong-doing, which never fails to come in the quiet time, and the confession which follows in the sharing time.

Recently I spent an evening with a group of little girls which a teacher in a large private school in the country has started. The girls are from the tiny village, consisting almost entirely of people who work in or for some department of the school, or from "the Flats," a district down by the river, where the people are the families of rough workmen in the quarries or the stone-crusher.

They all entered earnestly into quiet time, one girl even having paper and pencil to write what came to her. When sharing time came, one little girl, named Pauline, broke out impulsively, "I had a terrible fight with brother today and I gave him a good licking." This, she said, had come to her in the quiet time to confess. Mental struggle was evident in her face, however, and Miss F., the leader, waited a moment. Then exclaimed Pauline, "But he started it and I'm going to give him another licking tomorrow!"

Conviction of sin, but no genuine repentance, was there and the child thoroughly understood it herself. A story was told ending with a boy's remark: "It's not your business what the other fellow does wrong; that's God's job. But it's your getting mad that makes God mad." Did those children who listened, did Pauline, understand individual responsibility for sin? I *know* they did. More prayer followed, and Pauline, when she left, said, "I won't hit brother tomorrow."

Two tiny tots in our church school kindergarten

sprang at each other one morning so viciously and with such screams that I went into the room. It was very early and the teacher had not yet arrived, but the children had been permitted to play in the room to prevent their wandering out in the street. It was difficult to separate them and still more difficult to understand what either was trying to say in accusation of the other. Both were from good homes and had all the care and training at home that mothers and nurses could give.

Finally I sat down between them and put my hand over my eyes to pray. Instinctively both little boys did the same thing. Nothing was said. In a few seconds one jumped up and, taking the other by the hand, said, "Jimmie, you can have the bells; let's play with them."

LYING

No problem in a home is generally so mishandled as children's "lies," as parents erroneously call them. Often a child is converted into a genuine and habitual liar because parents and teachers fail to trace the source of what seems to be lies or increase the habit by wrong methods of correction.

The source in a little child is usually imagination. The story he tells has been a real picture to him and he loves it so much that he wants others to know it and enjoy it with him. If he creates amusement and interest in his audience of grown-ups, his imagination is stimulated to greater effort in order that he may occupy the center of attention. If his parents fail to give his story the attention he feels it merits and use injudicious checking, he loses confidence in them and takes his stories to outsiders, to the humiliation of the parents and often unjust punishment for him.

I have always admired my sister's handling of one of her children, a little girl with a great imagination and an intensely loving nature, much younger than her sisters and living in a houseful of adults. My sister would listen attentively to little Emilie's stories and then she would say, "Mother loves that story," or, "That's a wonderful story, Emilie," and then, always with her arms around the child, "Now tell Mother what really, truly happened and who was really, truly there."

Sometimes the source of the falsehood is fear, not necessarily fear provoked by parent or adult, but unconscious fear provoked by no recognizable cause. Punishment increases the fears. Explanation is not understood. All that the child grasps is that for some mysterious reason he has displeased somebody, and he tells another untruth as an escape from a new, but known fear.

My visit in a friend's home once was completely spoiled by my distress over her wrong treatment of her little son when he took some forbidden candy. Discovering not only the loss from the box, but also the traces of chocolate on his chubby little face, she called, "Tommie, did you take my candy?" Promptly came the answer, "No, no, Mummy."

Catching him by the arm and shaking him, the mother said: "Tommie, I will not have you lie like that. You must tell me the truth when I ask you a question. Now you have lied again, and in front of Aunt Olive!"

For fifteen minutes a weeping mother, more angry every minute, and a puzzled, stolid little boy faced each other. To every repetition of the question, "Now, Tommie, tell me the truth, did you take that candy?" came in reply, a stubborn denial which finally became a hangdog shake of his head, always negative. I did not want to interfere, for that would have an effect on the child almost as bad as the scene which had already occurred, but I could not permit the threatened whipping, and so I said:

"Ellen, suppose you and Tommie and I have a quiet time together before you whip him. Maybe God will help Tommie to tell you who took the candy."

Ellen was not then accustomed to our quiet-time practice, but she sensed disapproval in my manner and was probably glad, also, to have an excuse not to give the whipping. So we bowed our heads. The silence grew so long that our four-year-old Tommie concluded the matter was ended and went out to play. Then Ellen and I had a long talk together to search out and learn to avoid in the future the many complexes and conflicts she had been developing in his mental make-up.

To begin with, her very first question was wrong. Never, *never*, *never* ask a little child a question which can be answered by yes or no. Almost always he will answer the one he thinks will please you or the one which is prompted by fear. Truth does not enter into it, and he does not understand what is meant by either truth or falsehood. Approval, love, fear, these are the only motives he has, and these are subconscious. Right and wrong are standards requiring judgment, and Tommie had several years to go before that stage would be reached in either his ethical life or his training. Ellen should have phrased her question so that Tommie would have needed several sentences, a long story for a four-year-old, in the course of which he would inevitably have told the truth or at least have betrayed himself. Then mother and son could have faced the real problem, disobedience. To illustrate: "Tommie, how much of my candy did you take?" or, "Tommie, what did you do with the candy you took out of my box?" The direct question she used was really a temptation to lie, to seek approval falsely, to evade blame, thus instilling practices which provide conduct problems all through life.

Then the oft-repeated question! What could Tommie do but stick to his original denial? Could he possibly be caught out, "in front of Aunt Olive," in taking that candy? Ellen knew the truth, and her first question having failed to bring confession, she should have asked another, differently phrased, or better still, she might have taken the little boy aside and by a quiet, simple telling why she knew, she might have secured his confession and repentance.

There are other psychological factors involved in that story, but you must discover them for yourself, as this chapter is concerned only with the problem of what to do about children's lies. Ellen makes no such mistakes today, for she takes God to guide her methods of discipline, and both she and Tommie have learned the secret of the quiet time.

As already stated, many of the stories in this book,

told to illustrate concretely how some childhood problem may be readily solved, have been written to me by parents wonderfully coöperative when I requested permission to use some incident I knew or had witnessed among their children. Sometimes they have been so vividly related that it seems best to quote their own language. The next story is one such story and it emphasizes the value of the quiet time in correcting children's faults and training right habits, especially the habit of truth-telling.

"The use of guidance in our house has very greatly assisted in solving the problems of a moral character which must invariably arise during the training of any child. In a household containing three children of widely differing characteristics it has proved invaluable as a means of harmonizing conflicting desires.

"Aged eight, Mary was a very imaginative child, often controlled by her imagination seemingly to the point of not distinguishing between truth and fiction. The circumstances of the household were these: there were no financial problems of a nature to cause the child any uncertainty; she had a plentiful supply of pretty things, books, toys, and so forth, the books being especially beloved. The household consisted of her grandfather, her parents, two younger sisters, a nurse, and two other maids. There was occasionally present a godson of her father's, a somewhat irresponsible person who was preparing for college and who about this time ran away from school two or three times because he could not bring himself to submit to consecutive discipline. He occasioned us much trouble and anxiety, though he was a sweet-tempered boy and devoted to the children, who were fond of him.

"At Christmas time he went one day to bring one of them home from school. They were strict at the school as to whom the teachers should consign children. The headmistress, seeing this boy, spoke to Mary's teacher and said to her, 'Who is that boy that Mary is going home with?' to which the child's special teacher replied, 'That is one of her brothers.' The headmistress looked surprised and said, 'Why, she has no brothers!' The child's own teacher said, 'Yes, she has three; they are all away in boarding-school. One of them, named Paul, is giving them a great deal of trouble. He is disagreeable in the family, he has run away from school several times, and they are very unhappy about him. The other two occasion them no anxiety.' The headmistress was obliged to explain that she knew the family, that Mary was the eldest, and that she had two little sisters, and no brothers whatever. The room teacher was amazed at the scope of the child's imagination and the skill with which she used it. Naturally, the parents were informed at once. The child had shown signs of lying before, but never on this scale. Her mother had made distinct efforts to make the child distinguish between a story told as a story, and the truth. Naturally the family was much distressed, especially as the child attempted to deny to the parents that she had ever done any such thing. When faced with the fact that they felt obliged to believe her teacher rather than herself, she was very much troubled, but was inclined still to be stubborn about it.

"The parents, at their wits' end, decided that it would be well to consult the local mental-hygiene bureau, which was remarkably well staffed, but no appointment could be secured for some days. Obviously the matter could not be allowed to rest in abeyance, and they proceeded to have a quiet time about it, at first without the child and then with her. So far the parents, the child, and the two teachers were the only ones who knew of the matter. At the end of it they came to the following conclusions: They decided that it should go no farther, with the exception of the person at the mental-hygiene bureau. It was further decided that Mary, who admitted her wrong-doing, should be punished.

"The question was, how? Spanking seemed altogether unsuitable. Disgrace of some kind seemed likely to make matters worse. The thing that came to us both, which the child agreed to, was that everything not necessary to the child's existence should be taken away from her—her toys and books, everything she enjoyed most and used. She had a great many things of which she was very fond. They were all taken away, entirely out of her room. For every day that she could say there had been no misstatement of any kind, she was to earn one thing back. For large things, such as her dolls' house, she must work a week. She was permitted to choose the thing she would have. This was immediately put into practice.

"Four days later she was taken down to the mental-hygiene bureau. There the man in charge had some conversation with her. She was then sent to play downstairs and he proceeded to talk to us. We explained what had happened. He told us what she had told him, which was more of the same type of thing that she had told at school, though in a different line, and having more basis in fact. He said to us: 'Obviously you have done something about this. What have you done?' We told him. He seemed very much astonished, and said to us, 'Do you mean to say that not even the child's grandfather nor her nurse know anything about this?' We said no, that it seemed to us that it was none of their business, and that if she did wrong, she ought to know that she could trust us as well as when she did right. He said, 'This is amazing; it is perfectly ideal.' We told him about the punishment and that the child had agreed to it. He said: 'It is perfect. How did you arrive at such conclusions?' He was obviously not a religious man, so we explained to him that we had spent a good while trying to find out what would be the best way to deal with her, and this was what had come to both of us. He said, 'If you can only stick to this program, you ought to have excellent results. Come back in eight weeks and bring the child.' Nothing more was said.

"At the end of the eight weeks we went back with her again, and he had some small conversation with her, and then came to us. 'What have you to report?' he asked. We told him that, checking up with each other and the teacher, as far as we could judge there had been only once when she had deliberately lied. Several times at first she had started one of her fabrications, and had checked herself and told the truth. Only once in all that time had she forgotten. 'How many of her things,' he asked, 'has she earned back?' We were able to reply that she had gotten back virtually everything. He was very much pleased, and it has never been necessary to go back.

"In the last three years there have been times when we have been obliged to remind her of that episode, and to make her realize that the truth must be told at any cost. She has a tendency to exaggerate and to make up stories, but they are never of a nature to cause any trouble. She is becoming thoroughly reliable whenever questions of fact arise, and when she is difficult to deal with in such ways, we try always to have a quiet time with her. She is much less prone to lament the injustices of some seemingly drastic punishment if we have a quiet time about it together, and the times requiring punishment are much less frequent than seems to be the case in other families.

"She and her next sister come regularly to quiet time before breakfast every morning. It is interesting to observe how frequently their guidance is of a constructive nature. They do not always get anything very definite, but repeatedly the indolent child says in the sharing time: 'It comes to me not to be lazy. I must do . . .' mentioning some particular thing which is not according to her nature otherwise. And the fussy child who has the tendency to nag says, 'I must not be fussy; I must not tease; I must not bother with the little ones.'

"As yet the little ones do not come regularly to quiet time with the family. They have a shorter one better suited to their years with their nurse. The five-year-old is very eager to join the family quiet time, but the three-year-old finds it hard to sit still for long enough, and feels left out if he is not allowed to come, too. Our method is usually to read something from the Bible, usually the New Testament, and sometimes, if the passage is obscure, there are questions to bring out the meaning. Then we have a time of quiet. Whoever reads the Bible closes the quiet time with prayer, and we share what came to us in the quiet time. Mary has a quiet time of her own frequently, but when she does she is apt to miss the group quiet time and it does not seem to be so profitable for her. We need each other, and it has become obvious to us that the group is greater than the individual."

FEAR

Mead's mother, Virginia, had herself to learn a long, hard lesson in the conquest of fear, and she resolved early to help Mead face the problem in his own life while still a little boy. She was influenced again in this respect by another mother, equally desirous for her child's freedom from fear, whose methods had failed. There was enlightenment as to the cause of this mother's failure in her remark to Virginia: "Of course I'm an awful coward myself, but I never let Marie see it, and she says to me, 'Mother, it must be wonderful to be as brave as you are.' "

In contrast to this, Virginia's guidance was, constantly: "Share with Mead, share your problems where you turn for help, how you get victory." She obeyed, using each opportunity as it came along. Once it would be the doing of something she did not want to do and showing how God made her willing to go ahead. Young as he was, he caught the implied comparison with himself and how he might become willingly obedient when Mummy or Daddy required something contrary to his own wishes.

A most interesting incident occurred in relation to physical fear. Virginia had to take fifteen inoculations for hay fever to prevent the recurrence of the annual summer attack. She dreaded them, really physically afraid of pain. Mead was three and a half years old. Virginia told him of her fear and asked him to pray with her. He was thrilled to be asked to help Mummy! Each time Virginia went to the doctor's office, they prayed, and Mead would say:

"Dear Jesus, please help Mummy so she won't cry. Now, Mummy, you won't be afraid, because I said a prayer for you."

Sometimes he went with her, saw the inoculation performed, and saw the result of their prayer.

Faith, prayer, sharing, had their effect on his own courage, the following year, when he himself had to have a slight operation. To his father's amazement, Mead, who had been fearful of anything done to him, showed no sign of fear of hospital, ether, nurse, or doctor. His only remark was: "Why doesn't that doctor come? I can't wait any longer."

At five and a half, Mead faced another fear and gained victory again through his faith in "listening" to God's direction to him in the quiet time. For a long time Mead had a most curious fear of anything new. It showed itself in doing new things, in seeing a new kind of machinery like a cider mill, and particularly in putting on unfamiliar clothes. Trying on shoes, coats, or hats was a tragedy to him and a humiliation to his mother. He would never "dress up" in paper hats or costumes. One time, when Virginia took him to see her cousin, an orthopedic doctor, to have his feet examined, a terrible scene ensued. Because he had to take off his shoes and socks he fell into a fit of crying that sounded as if he had lost his last friend and were being lashed with a whip as well. Persuasion, explanation, and punishment availed not at all in allaying his fear, the real source of which was undiscoverable.

Then came school days. This idea appealed to his pride in being a big boy, and at first his fear of the new was forgotten. But the old fear returned when his teacher talked of plans for Mead to paint pictures. It was something new, and he was to wear a smock, another new thing. No thrill! just fear of these awful, strange things, paint and smock. Each morning Mead would say, quite casually, that he guessed he wouldn't go to school that day. Virginia and his father understood. No discussion, no objection, but somehow he always went.

The fourth morning, as Mead and Han (the father) were on their way to school, Mead said:

"Daddy, I'm not going to be afraid of painting."

"That's fine," said Han. "How did that happen?"

Mead replied, "I had a little quiet time this morning, all by myself, and Jesus told me it was silly to be afraid of new things, and so I'm not."

He painted that day. During the week-end, he tried

on five new summer suits, put on a paper hat. A week or so later, he tried on several pairs of shoes. Several weeks later he went to the doctor for a thorough examination, and though he suggested that his young sister be examined first, when he arrived, he very happily and willingly had all his clothes removed.

His mother's comment carries a whole sermon on child-training—"I have always shared with him, even my own fears, and the way God can help us."

I cannot resist telling an amusing sequel which came to my knowledge later in the summer, when he and his cousin Skippy, about the same age, were together at the family country home. There are two girls among the cousins, younger than the boys. One of them, Anne, is a lovable little tomboy, who not only adores her brother Skippy, but has always played with him and Mead. This summer, Mead's newly found appreciation of being a "real big boy" no longer overcome by shameful fear, created in him a desire to leave the girls out of the games he and Skippy invented, and masculine solidarity began with the two boys.

Said the new Mead: "Ah, we don't want girls. They're always *afraid*."

Despite the hint of a new problem thus introduced for Virginia, Han, and Mead to share and solve together, the incident indicates how complete is his victory over his own fear. And, up to date, Anne has blocked all efforts at her own exclusion!

Marshall's father is a clergyman. Both he and his wife have a living faith in God. From the very beginning of Marshall's life, long before his actual coming to this earth, they shared with each other their hopes for his Christian character and how they would work together to develop it. Both are now also active believers in the message of the Oxford Group and in the efficacy of sharing and of the quiet time.

Their efforts to guide Marshall into a sense of real prayer show how truly and closely a very little child may learn to know God.

From the time he was old enough to form words they taught him to talk to Jesus, and they tried to give him an idea of who Jesus was and what he could mean to a very little child. There came a period (he was a little over three) when his prayers were a perfect farce. He belonged to the peripatetic school of pray-ers and as like as not would take a dive under his crib to pull the cat's tail while they were kneeling in prayer.

When H. was in Louisville, with an Oxford Group team of workers, she asked Marshall's parents if they had quiet times with Marshall. They told her that they had prayers with him, but that they could hardly call them *quiet* times. The mother doubted whether a child of Marshall's tender years and dynamic and impulsive disposition could have a quiet time in this stage of his development.

It was just about then that Marshall began to show the first signs of fear of the dark and of going to bed. His favorite book was *Peter Rabbit*. In it there is a picture of the long-bearded Mr. McGregor on his hands and knees planting young cabbages. In our edition the printing is faulty and the beard completely submerges the hungry farmer's mouth. This picture was particularly fascinating to Marshall, who would shudder with nervous glee and exclaim, "Him got no mouth!" And yet he put little rabbits in pies! Truly an eerie phenomenon. And as Marshall would wriggle into his crib at night he would squeal, "Ooo! Mr. McGregor will git me!"

It seemed that now it certainly could do no harm to have a quiet time with Marshall and that it might help eradicate his incipient fears. So they told him that the loving, gentle Jesus is always near him and that if we close our eyes and listen quietly he will speak to us. This was fun, and it was friendly for Daddy and Mother to share what Jesus had told them. It was when they had that first quiet time that Marshall declared, very positively: "Jesus loves Marsie, and he won't let Mr. McGregor put him in a pie."

That was the end of night terror and of unwillingness to go to bed, and the fear of Mr. McGregor has never returned. Young as he is, Marshall can listen to Jesus as well as a grown-up, and Jesus gives him as real direction as he gives to his parents.

SELFISHNESS

Day's real sin was selfishness, although its outward manifestation was quarreling. She had a great many toys, books, beads, playthings of all sorts, and she lived in a beautiful house in the country. For nearly two years she was the only baby in the home and by the time little sister Florence came along, or was old enough to play with her, Day had developed a keen sense of ownership and definite unwillingness to share possessions with anyone. She would not let Florence play with her toys or even touch any of her belongings. When other children came to play, quarreling was constant.

Connie, the mother, and Nell, the governess, were greatly troubled by Day's attitude and frequently prayed together, asking God to show them how to meet the problem. Guidance came to them to tell Day stories which brought out the idea of sharing and of unselfish giving. They trusted her to make her own application, and it worked, even to the extent of her finding out for herself that sharing toys might mean breakage, the loss to be borne good-naturedly.

After a while, frank talks between child and governess became possible and their quiet times often revealed how God was guiding the little girl better and farther than did any teaching or moralizing. Several instances are worth telling, especially as they indicate the relationship which must first exist between parent or teacher and the child before either can be open to God's guidance.

Nell had a bracelet which Day greatly admired and often asked for. Nell had always refused, fearing damage by baby hands. In one quiet time it came to Nell to say to Day:

"I've been selfish in not allowing you to play a few minutes with my bracelet. It has made Jesus unhappy. I'm sorry."

No comment was made at the time, no effort to point a lesson. But in succeeding quiet times Day would say:

"Jesus says that I was selfish with my toys today and that I must let Florence play with them."

Or, "Jesus says that Florence is selfish with her doll. I must teach her not to be, because it makes Jesus unhappy."

Again, "Dear Jesus, I'm sorry I was selfish with Gray" (a frequent playmate). And, "Jesus says that when Gray comes tomorrow, I'm to let her have my hoop."

Gradually, Day changed, often offering her best-loved toys to Florence and saying, "If you break it, it doesn't matter, because you don't know any better."

Sometimes she could be heard passing on to Florence the new idea she was learning herself, "Don't do that, Florence; it makes Jesus unhappy when we are selfish."

As Christmas time approached, Connie's guidance gave her another method of helping Day to overcome selfishness, so often and so sorrowfully produced in children in wealthy families by the numerous Christmas gifts. She began to tell Day stories of children who were cold or hungry, or had no toys, or had no little sister to play with. At night they prayed for the child Day heard about from her mother. Then one night she looked up and said:

"Mummy, Jesus wants me to give that poor little girl my sheep."

Each night she told of some gift, a toy of her own, that she was to send some "poor little girl" for Christmas. At first the gifts were discarded toys, things she no longer played with, but finally her quiet times brought this message:

"Jesus says to give my big kitty (a toy kitty with which she slept every night) to the poor children, 'cause they can snuggle against it and keep warm."

On Christmas morning, in the middle of opening her own presents, she stopped and said:

"I'll bet the poor children are having fun today with their presents, too." She had helped, the day before, in packing a box of gifts for the church to distribute.

Recently she began to pray for her playmates and to explain to them how Jesus is showing her how to be unselfish.

TEMPER

Temper is another undesirable attribute children manifest early and with no known cause except self-will. It often begins in tiny babyhood, and wrong treatment or indifference in babyhood establishes in many a child the habit of breaking out into rages and angry crying whenever wishes are opposed. The problem of discipline has begun in a family when the baby screams to have his own way and has become really serious the first time his baby tongue says, "I won't," or, "I don't want to."

This problem of temper caused Connie and Nell considerable anxiety. Unaware of its importance in such a young child, the parents had not done much about it at first, hoping that she would "grow out of it" as she left babyhood behind. But she did not. Instead, the tempers increased in frequency.

Their prayers in quiet time brought to Connie and

Nell the plan of putting Day into her room, alone, with the door closed, and with the suggestion that she spend the time in asking Jesus to help her stop her angry screaming. At first there were some real battles so that the nerves and faith of Connie and Nell were sorely tried. Then one day a long silence came instead of crying, and Day remarked, as they opened the door,

"I was going to get into a rage, but Jesus told me that if I did I'd just have to stay longer. So I didn't!"

In her quiet time that night she shared, "Jesus said it made him unhappy when I was so cross and mean."

That she recognizes her acts of temper as wrongdoing and suffers real conviction when she falls into a rage is evidenced by these quotations from her quiet-time sharing:

"I can hardly wait to finish my bath, I want to talk to Jesus so much."

"Jesus, please help me not to do things I shouldn't do and not to touch things I shouldn't touch."

"Florence, you mustn't tear up my books any more. Jesus says it's mean, but he says I mustn't get angry at you."

"Jesus says I must tell Mummy how bad I was today."

This is no abnormal child, nor even a precocious one. I have spent many happy hours in her home and I know she is just a happy, active little girl. She is unusually blessed in parents whose training of their children is guided by their faith in God and by their earnest personal study of their children's needs, spiritually as well as material. Nor is there the slightest priggishness, or any danger of it. When God and Jesus are not words reserved for church (a queer, mysterious place adults send children on Sundays!) but mean a living, natural element in the daily life of a home, religion is as free from priggishness as talk of dolls or daisies.

"BAD" LANGUAGE

"Bad" language is still another problem, the use of which in the homes of the children of careful parents can only be prompted by original sin! The source may be traced to street or school playmates, but *why* do children "pick up" bad language so readily and cling to it in spite of the home environment? And what can you do about it?

The Wishard family faced the issue not long ago. They live in a small suburban town and the children, Frances and Van, played with neighborhood children, no slum neighborhood by any means, either. Helen, the mother, returning after an absence, heard with shock and alarm the two little ones call each "Sap" and "Dirty skunk" when the argument seemed to call for strong terms. Listening more carefully afterward, she heard in remarks they exchanged with each other, as well as with others as the practice grew, such expressions as "Fresh face," "Nut," "Rotter," and even "damn" and "Go to hell."

Inquiry followed. The maid said that she couldn't imagine where they learned such language, but that she had done her best to stop it, for she had washed out their mouths with soap every time she heard it. Good, old-fashioned punishment, but the only effect it had was that the next time either child was cross with the maid both of them called her the worst name they had been punished for using!

Expostulation and example also failed. Frances and Vannie just could not see why they should not use terms which so aptly expressed their feelings at the moment. Helen was needed away from home again and she asked Nell, the governess of Day's story, to stay with the children and to concentrate her attention on correcting their language habits. Nell soon learned the situation for herself, for in a day or two Frances exclaimed over some tiny injury after a fall: "This hurts, Aunt Nell, honest to God it does. Honest to God!"

In her own quiet time she prayed earnestly for God to show her the way to cure the two little ones of their unfortunate speech-habits in such a way that they would understand the sin and therefore be induced to self-effort. It came to her to begin with Frances and to use the phrase, "It hurts Jesus," which Day had understood and applied. Frances knew about quiet times, for her father and mother often prayed and shared with her. So she was willing to listen when Nell explained to her about the words and names she called, saying:

"You see, Frances, it hurts Jesus when you use mean words. Wouldn't you rather be like Aunt Margery and love Jesus so much that you won't say anything to hurt him?" Two intimate friends of the parents, also workers in the Oxford Group, are named Margery and adored by Frances.

She thought for a while, wanted to know why her words hurt Jesus, and decided she would try to "talk like Aunt Margery." In a later quiet time she prayed, "Dear Jesus, please help me not to say . . ." (a list of bad words and names that startled Aunt Nell). The next night, after the quiet time, she said:

"Jesus says I was much better today and he's happy. I only said 'sap' once and 'fresh face' once. But Jesus says we ought to do something about Vannie; he's terrible!"

So they decided that Frances should help Vannie. Next morning, at breakfast, she told Vannie she was going to help him not to say "those words because they make Jesus unhappy." Each night she asked Jesus to help her not to say mean words, and to help Vannie, too. Within ten days all such words were no longer used by Frances, even in temper, and Van had improved also. Helen, the mother, wrote Nell weeks afterward that Frances had not used one wrong word, and Van's only fall was in calling some one a skunk!

CHAPTER V

PRODIGAL PARENTS

IN THIS chapter our attention is to be concentrated on one particular type of parent. There is no implication that the prodigal parent is a universal type. History, as well as our personal experience, gives too many instances of consecrated mothers and wise fathers, and one of the positive indications that we are entering upon a new and better era in religion and in education is the change in the attitude of young parents today, their sense of responsibility, their earnest seeking for knowledge and direction, the increased time and thought they give personally to the little ones whose destiny rests on their decisions.

Nevertheless, the *prodigal* parent has marred many a young life and must bear, more than any one other influence, the blame for the pagan and selfish conduct and point of view of youth since the war. Unhappily, few of these prodigal parents recognize themselves as such, hence this chapter.

For at least two generations, parents and teachers have been mutually accusatory in their placing of blame for the failures of youth when confronted with the actual problems of life. Being "organization" driven, we have made sporadic efforts at coöperation between these two peoples, mainly responsible for youth's training, by means of joint associations, meetings, magazines, and what not. All steps in the right direction, doubtless, but generally they left out the two most important elements, namely, God and the child himself. The guidance of God and the coöperation of the child were seldom really and truly sought.

Adult will and adult ideas, usually unexplained by parent and teacher, even more often misunderstood by the child and deeply offensive to his notions of justice and self-respect, naturally bring about a clash with the child and a "discipline problem" results. Temper, sullenness, unwilling submission, secret resentment, and a secret setting of the child's will to be free as soon as he dares and to deceive those who have thus imposed authority upon him, this is the inevitable progression in the psychology of the youth. The parent and teacher, confronted with such a situation, the fruits of their own sowing, resort to sternness, harsh and peremptory commands, punishment. Fear is the only motive made active in the child. Love and confidence vanish. Barriers are set up between the child and God, child and parents, which in later years can be broken down with great difficulty, possibly never, unless the principles of surrender to God, guidance, and sharing become known to one or both.

Many of the stories already told in this book clearly illustrate how the quiet time and the sharing which follows it have solved the discipline problem in many homes. The story of Charlie affords specific illustration. Listen to it.

Charlie, aged fourteen, lived with his grandfather

and his grandfather's second wife, his step-grandmother. Domestic tragedies had brought about this unusual home for a boy. Two generations of thought and time separated him from his grandfather. His cousin, as he called his step-grandmother, although younger, had no ties of kinship and few of sympathy with his little life. He was not a very welcome addition to the home. He incarnated the family tragedy and necessitated duties and obligations his elders had finished with years before.

Nor was he a nice boy. Far from it. He had few attractive qualities and more than the usual boy's dislike for washing hands and face. Repeated chiding, and even sending from the dinner table because of his dirt and untidiness, had no effect. His impertinence, disobedience, and annoying behavior were beyond description, and it were wiser to leave his language untold.

His grandparents were completely discouraged. The home was very unhappy. The grandparents were sincerely pious, church-going people. They tried to give religious instruction to the boy, but it made no appeal. He scorned it and everything relating to religion. Sternness from the one and injustice and impatience from the other grandparent, combined with the dim understanding he probably had that his parents were not like those his playmates had, darkened his young soul. His only defense was to annoy and be disagreeable.

Then the Groups came to his town. His grandfather, a leader in the community, welcomed them. He sought for himself and his friends the new release and new vision of spiritual experience the teachings of the Groups brought. His wife, Charlie's step-grandmother, was one of the first to surrender her life and her will to God.

Two days later she asked the boy to sit down with her, she had something to tell him. She shared with him the story of her impatience, asked him to forgive her, and assured him that she did love him. The boy replied: "I knew by your face that you got this the day after they came here, but you did not give it to me until two days later. I'd *like* to have a quiet time with you."

Many quiet times together followed. Pages from his guidance book, which he permitted some of us to read, show how in these succeeding quiet times the Holy Spirit convicted him of faults often uselessly corrected by his elders, some unknown and never confessed to them before. Ten days later, he said to his step-grand-mother, after a quiet time with her: "I really love you now. I love you more than my bugle." The full value of this statement will be recognized when one knows that his ambition just then was to be a soldier, and the bugle represented it all.

Nor was this effort at a new method of discipline a ten days' wonder, a mere flash in the pan, as it were. Charlie has carried on faithfully, applying his new idea of sharing and guidance in all his relationships, and has recently united with the church in which his grandparents are leading members.

Probably one of the most baffling problems, unless the mother seeks and obeys the guidance of God and has established a habit of quiet time, prayer, and mutual sharing, is that of the relationship between the adolescent girl and her mother. I know a woman whose whole sex thought and social life were shadowed for many years by her mother's failure to share honestly at a most critical point in her girlhood. The girl was just beginning to attend parties with boys and was very popular. She was intelligent, even intellectual, and had considerable ability in writing articles for her church and college journals.

After the publication of an unusually clever article of hers, an anonymous letter was sent to the editor of the church magazine where it had appeared. The letter stated bluntly and crudely that the girl was an illegitimate child, that her parents had not married until she was nearly a year old, and that the marriage was even then of doubtful legality, as the mother's first husband had never been divorced and the parents had relied on the statutory limitation in regard to the disappearance of the husband before a wife may marry again. The editor, a very young man and a malicious joker, read the letter aloud in the presence of the girl and several of her associates.

Wild with anger, the girl snatched the letter out of his hands and went home with it to her mother. Something in the mother's face and her first involuntary utterance, "This is Blank's work," told the girl that the letter said the truth. She listened in stunned silence as her mother talked threats of what must be done to find and punish the author of such a scurrilous attack. She interrupted once to say: "Mamma, if it's true, tell me. I will love you just the same." The mother's reply,

"How dare you even ask that question?" ended the incident.

The moment for confidence and loving sharing between mother and daughter was lost and never reestablished. The rest of the story cannot be given here, for the woman is living and well known, but the best years of her youth were tragedies which might have been spared if her mother had been honest with her then.

A happier story is that of a little girl of thirteen who recently attempted her first flirtation, her first "petting party." Like many a girl, she had no serious intention of wrong-doing. It was merely experimentation in a new field of knowledge. Long accustomed to quiet times with father and mother, she listened for guidance the next morning, and during the sharing time she said, "Mummy, God tells me I have something to share with you." Alone together later, mother heard the story of the night before without scolding and without evidence of shock. In their later quiet time, the girl told God aloud that she was sorry for being so silly, and—absolved the boy from all blame! Can we doubt that this girl's mother will never grieve over loss of her daughter's confidence and that the girl will never seek other confidantes, saying: "I can't tell mother. She never understands"?

Recently, a mother and daughter of nineteen or twenty both attended some Group meeting in the city where they were temporarily living. A barrier had arisen between the two, although the home was usually a very happy one, with little or no conflict. The surrender of her will to Christ was made first by Ada, the daughter. Her quiet-time guidance was to tell her mother that she did not want to go to college, that she liked boys and wanted to go out and have a good time and not study. The mother, Mrs. K., wept over the ingratitude of a girl who was willing to throw away her opportunities, and the barrier remained.

Later Mrs. K. came into a new knowledge of Christ's power to guide, and quiet times and sharing together became part of the daily life in the home. One day Mrs. K. shared with Ada the ambitious hopes the parents had for the girl and her brothers, said that she was sorry she had never consulted the girl's own wishes, and that her guidance was to ask Ada to decide for herself.

A long and amusing time of complete sharing followed. All the little irritations each had felt against the other were told and laughed over. Ada shared her fear of being an "old maid," her desire for home and children rather than a career, and her jealousy of her mother's attractiveness and calm ease in company. Mrs. K. shared her distaste for Ada's new addiction to most pronounced make-up with rouge and lipstick and her fear of Ada's being man-crazy.

The barriers are all broken down. A happy solution which satisfies both came simultaneously in the guidance of quiet time, and both are zealously working to win souls for Christ.

Recently a mother told me, with tears and uncontrollable emotion, the story of her failure to give any religious teaching to her son in his childhood and of his reproach to her for this lack in his life. In the years that have passed since, the mother has found God and has had a real and very vital spiritual experience. She entered into active work for Christ in the Fellowship "groups" and became greatly desirous that her loved ones should have the love of Christ in their hearts, too.

She talked with her sons and other members of her family, telling them the marvelous new joy and peace which she had discovered. She tried to live before them according to the new principles of Christ-centered living she was learning. They noticed and commented on the marked change in her attitude and on the many ways in which her daily life was sweeter and truer. One day, after she had spoken to her older son about his seeking to find this same spiritual reality, he said, in loving, but yet definite reproach:

"Mother, I am twenty-six years old now and it is too late for me to learn belief in God. You left something out of my life when I was a child, the right time for me to learn and experience it. You never sent me to Sunday school. You never taught me to pray. I never heard you pray or talk about prayer when I was a boy. I have grown up with no knowledge of spiritual facts, if there are any, and my philosophical studies give me no certainty. I am an agnostic and I cannot believe. Maybe I might have."

The mother shared with her boy the great sorrow that entered her life with his father's untimely death before he was born and the struggles she, herself only a very young woman, had gone through during the period of his infancy and early childhood. She told how she had turned against God in her resentment and bitterness and had taught herself to believe that there could be no good God that would permit such things to be. He listened sympathetically as he is a good man and a loving son. But God and the divine sacrifice made by Christ are incomprehensible to him.

Of course, at twenty-six there is no such thing as never or too late, and the mother's prayers and faith will be answered by God in His own good time. Meantime this young man is teaching other youths philosophy. Can we wonder that we have college boys and girls leaving their institutions of learning with faith destroyed and selfish individualism controlling their destinies?

Attend, ye mothers and fathers who say that you will not influence your child's religious life and that it must be his own choice. Let him choose his doctrinal creed and his mode of church organization if you wish, for neither is basic to the reality of the spiritual life, but teach him to know God in prayer and in guidance. Else not only the reproach of this twenty-six-year-old lad may be yours, but the dire tragedy that usually awaits a life with no God-given standards.

The sin of possessiveness makes about as many prodigal parents as any I know. It begins in the child's babyhood, when parents in their pride and joy begin to plan the child's life for him from the cradle to the grave. It is often unconscious and is called love, protective measures, and other self-delusive names. Fathers are as guilty as mothers, even though they don't so often get caught out at it.

Mr. J. has a big family of children, and up to the time of his own surrender to Christ was absolutely possessive of every one of them. Sally, the oldest girl, was sent to learn to teach; Jim, the oldest boy, to a naval academy. The next girl, Helen, was selected to be the housekeeper and mother's assistant. Arthur, the next boy, was to learn farming and take care of that end of the father's business. And so on. No regard was paid to what might be their own choice of life work. Their fees and bills were all paid generously, they had good clothes, and had membership in good clubs, Boy Scouts, and so on, according to their age. But they had not one penny to spend as they pleased and without accounting to their father. This was not meanness, but lack of trust in their judgment of things and failure to see that they must learn independence and self-reliance even if by error.

As they grew older and inevitably less submissive to watching and direction, disruption happened in the home. Helen, the housekeeper daughter, showed great musical talent and was determined on developing it. The mother aided in deceiving the father and used marketing money for the girl's lessons. Sally shirked her studies so that the training-school authorities decided she was unfit to be a teacher, especially as she was so frequently away on unexplained absences, afterward discovered to be late parties at rather questionable roadhouses. Again the mother had shielded the girl from the father's wrath, until the time came that Sally was sent home. Even then mother and Sally planned how to deceive father about the dancing parties, dancing being rigidly forbidden by Mr. J.

Jim did well at the naval academy, but Arthur, at the time I first knew the family, was a veritable demon of a boy, the town terror. The long example of deceiving father and of success in secret defiance had inspired him to an earlier and more open defiance. He had been expelled from two schools and the aid of psychiatrists had been appealed to. My advice, as an expert with delinquent boys, was sought.

Then Mr. J. read a book[1] which convicted him of sin. He realized that all his religion was fear, and not love. He saw that God asks more than outward conformity to ceremony and commandments, that God asks us to live as guided by Him rather than by human will, and that all his own relationships had been governed by self-will and human planning. Soon after he heard that the Groups, in which the book's author was a leader, would hold meetings in the house of an acquaintance in the town. He attended and came into a rich, releasing experience of Christ's power to change his life. He shared fully with his wife and had the joy of seeing her also give her life to Christ and unite with him in the effort to rebuild their home.

The next step was more difficult, but it worked! One morning, the first opportunity he could get with the whole family assembled at family prayers, he shared with them his new experience. He told them his regret for his many years of unreasonable authority, his angry refusal to give consideration to their own wishes, the

[1] "Children of the Second Birth," by Rev. S. M. Shoemaker, Jr.

whole story. They listened in astonishment, silently, even sceptically at first, wondering what new dodge Dad was "putting over." Helen responded first and said she would like to go to some of those meetings— "they must be great."

Quiet times, with prayer and sharing and Bible passages appropriately chosen by each one as guided, took the place of the old long, unexplained, and uncomprehended chapter and tiresome "goody-goody" prayers. Confidence and coöperation took the place of long homilies and harsh rebuke. The girls and their mother confessed their long resentments and deceit. Happiness and peace reigned in that home instead of rebellion and discord.

The most extraordinary instance of a parent's realization, under the power of the Holy Spirit, that her possessiveness of her daughter was a sin came to my knowledge about two years ago. Mrs. H. was an able and indefatigable worker in her church and she could talk fluently and well on matters of religious doctrine. She was considered to be an exemplary Christian woman. In her home, however, a different story might have been told. Every circumstance, every interest, revolved around the daughter Anna, even to the discomfort and neglect of Mr. H., if his desires conflicted with Anna's needs as her mother saw them. Anna's health, Anna's clothes, Anna's friends, Anna's pleasures, every phase of the girl's life was watched over with a worrying care that exasperated the girl herself. Even family friends were made unwelcome unless they too worshiped at the same shrine or if a chance word of seeming comparison placed Anna in an inferior position. Irritation and revolt on the part of the girl and reproaches, fears, and tears on the part of the mother made the home unhappy and left Mr. H. a lonely, silent man.

At this stage in the family history, friends induced Mrs. H. to attend some meetings where she discovered that her own religious life had neither the certainty nor the radiance of those who spoke in witness of Christ's power in their lives. She had long, earnest talks, often lasting way into the night, with one woman friend whose life had been changed. Decision, even surrender to God of all she understood about herself, brought no peace. There was some barrier which she failed to see and which was not revealed to her friend. After a long night of sleeplessness and much prayer for God to show her the way and give her release, she arose and went down to breakfast, fairly well determined to give up the struggle and dismiss the whole thing from her mind.

She avoided her friend and sat outside on the porch on the other side of the house during the Group quiet time. But she was ill at ease, and, impelled against her will by a call stronger than her resolution, she went to the room where the Group was meeting. Bible study had just begun—the story of Abraham and Isaac. As the leader developed the thought that Abraham's faith in God was so great and so real that he was even willing to sacrifice his son, the greatly loved child of promise in his old age, she grasped her woman friend by the arm and pulled her out of the room.

Then she said: "My God! It's Anna! Anna is my

barrier to Christ." That was a difficult surrender to make, embracing the future as well as the past, fears as well as idolatrous love. But with radiant face and eyes that saw a vision, she wrote to her husband in confession of her neglect of him, assuring him that she did love him and would atone for the past. Letters went to relatives long ago offended and to Anna herself. A new life started in that home.

It is not yet a finished story. The alienated husband and the thoroughly spoiled girl have not yet themselves found Christ as a reality and a guide and are rather curiously watching the mother's progress, but it is certain and steady, directed by the Holy Spirit.

Fear of loss of respect from their children, and of consequent loss of control, brings about in many parents, especially fathers, a state of mind which reacts disastrously upon children of all ages, but particularly in late adolescence, that time of life when judgment is harsher and more final than it ever will be again. This fear makes parents lie and conceal, instead of making honest acknowledgment of their own errors. Even little children are not really deceived. A five-year-old boy said once: "Oh yes! I know Daddy was drunk last night, but you see he's my father and he's afraid to have me know, so he said he had a sick headache."

Norah Barton's parents were obsessed by this fear. Implicit obedience and unquestioning belief in their wisdom were demanded of her. Even as a tiny child she rebelled against them, not so much because of their authority as because she instinctively sensed that their private lives did not deserve the respect required.

"Don't tell your father I bought this hat," from mother, and, "Of course you're just like your mother, talking all the time," from father, inevitably led her to suspect them both and to take sides, sometimes one way, sometimes another. Both could not be allwise if they talked like that.

As she grew a little older she wanted pocket money. "That is for rich men's children," said father. "Your mother will buy you anything you must have." But mother was always too busy to go anywhere with Norah, even if Norah's companions would have waited for her while she went to find mother. So she learned to steal the stray cash her parents left lying on desk or bureau. Then suddenly she discovered that she was and always had been a rich man's child—one more lie added to the account she was mentally recording, an account which grew longer and heavier as the years passed.

Later came her début and new sources of conflicts with parents, more deceiving of them both, and reliance upon confidants outside the family circle, often unwisely chosen, often including men whose dancing abilities and flatteries blinded her to their faults and unsuitable companionship. At twenty she began to seek new thrills and ventured into very dangerous sex experiments. She had her own private bootlegger, transactions being carried on through her favorite "speakeasy," and she was generally recognized as belonging to a "fast set."

Father stormed and mother wailed. Her answer was a threat of a much debated and dreaded marriage if they did not let her "at last choose her own friends and pursuits," that she "knew her way about," that she was "thoroughly sick of fools and hypocrites," and that she was "the only honest person in the house, anyhow, whatever she did." A year in Europe with plenty of money to go where she pleased and buy what she liked, under the chaperonage of an aunt, was next tried. Before she left her home for this trip, which she accepted in full understanding that it was a bribe to bring good behavior, she said to her mother:

"Mother, I want you to know that it is of no use to take a holier-than-thou attitude with me any more. I have known for years that your continual quarreling with father was because he was unfaithful to you and that you pretended not to know it because of his money. Do you remember my asking you once what some one meant by the words, 'She is his mistress'? I had just overheard some one say that about father and Miss D. I was old enough to be told the truth, but you put me off with a silly excuse. So I watched and questioned among our friends until I found out the real facts. I have always known since then that you had no right to preach at me, either one of you."

Disaster and scandal marked Norah's life in the next three years. At last some one invited her to a Group house-party. She went half-unwillingly, partly out of boredom, partly intrigued by the change in a friend, ready, as she said, "to try anything once." It was the beginning of a new life for her, and she has become an influence which has brought a number of girls to seek and find God. Her most difficult surrender, she once said, was her contempt for her parents, and her most difficult restitution was sharing her story with them.

The more obviously prodigal parents, those who willfully and carelessly or heartlessly neglect their parental obligations, I have not been seeking to reach in the preceding pages of this chapter. It is to the less obviously prodigal parents that I appealed, those who by their sins of possessiveness, fear, and dishonesty, by their misguided conceptions of respect and discipline, and by their failure to seek God as their guide and to lead their children into the realities of spiritual experience, have achieved the same disastrous results as parents utterly ignorant or neglectful of their parental obligations.

It is of this latter type of parents I would speak now for a moment, for it has unfortunately increased in numbers. We are reaping, in their attitudes toward their children, the results of nearly two generations of false theories regarding the training of children, especially in social, religious, and ethical education.

Our emphasis on self-expression has developed a high degree of selfishness, self-will, and self-centeredness. We have forgotten that self-expression without discipline in childhood and without a social conscience and a social consciousness in manhood must inevitably and invariably be selfish in its manifestation. A generation, so trained, surrounded by the materialism and "get-rich-quick" ideals of the past fifty years, free to ignore or to question or to deny spiritual experience, untaught in spiritual law as the foundation for ethical and social truths, could but produce men and women who look lightly on parenthood and evade it in every particular when it interferes with their self-interest, whether in pleasure or in business.

Nor is the responsibility of parenthood met by money for physical care, clothes, and schooling, even if all of these be managed by the "best" people and in the "best" places. I know scores of parents grieving today over their children's failures in social conduct, directly traceable to their own neglect of the more intimate home training and influences which God-guided parental love might have given. A nurse in one family I know gave unstinted care to the health of the children intrusted to her, and the children are physically perfect. But the prayers she taught them to say were not only in a foreign language, but of a faith equally foreign to that of their family's inherited faith, and her remarks upon religion, often intentionally made in their presence, alienated them from their father, a clergyman. An expensive school, selected because the "right" people sent their girls there, has given to a girl I know charming manners (when she has her own way), a fair acquaintance with books, and a sparkling wit, but listen to her mother's tearful words when the girl returned home after an absence of two years, distance and finances having prevented more frequent visits!—"My God! what can I do with her? I'm ashamed to be seen on the street with her! And she laughed at her father for wanting her to go to church with him, saying *she* was neither an infant nor a hypocrite!"

His father a banker and his mother active in many clubs and social-service organizations, both parents church members in so far as pew-rental and "high holy-day" contributions make one religious, but otherwise thoroughly pagan, Gerald had every advantage money and social connections could give,—the "right" school and college, the "right" clubs, even the "right" marriage. Then at twenty-four he shocked his world by the publication at his own expense of a pamphlet both obscene and scurrilous in its attack on the church and its institutions, especially marriage, and cynically definite in defense of homosexuality. The real sinners, the ones God will hold responsible for his offenses—for there were many more to follow—are his parents. That father knew more intimately the men in his clubs and bank than he did his own son, whom he regarded as first, a "costly nuisance," later an "unlicked cub whom his mother spoiled," and finally, a "degenerate ingrate, let him take his queer associates but keep out of my house." The mother sought aid from psychiatrists, new cults, even fortune-tellers, never God.

They were prodigal parents. They still are, for when the young wife found God as a guide, through her contact with the Oxford Group one summer, and attempted the rehabilitation of her home and her husband, they opposed vigorously her "extreme and unconventional views," although divorce and a homeless grandchild were the only other alternatives.

The word divorce brings me to the most unregenerate type of prodigal parent I can think of, the father or mother of children who consents to or seeks divorce lightly or for reasons of self-interest or personal happiness. There may be exceptions, but I have never known any child of divorced parents whose life was not shadowed, if fortunate enough to escape tragedy. A whole book the size of this one could be filled with stories of what has happened to children of divorced parents, the utter shattering of their faith in either parent or God, the cynicism with which they view sex and marriage, the futility they think lies in law or sacrament.

A college girl recently told me it did not matter whether she became a drunkard or a prostitute, as her father is the former and her mother is a prostitute legalized by three marriages and two divorces. An effort to save her by appeal to the father brought a reply from him, "She's her mother's daughter; she'd better go where the money is, as her mother did years ago." A later appeal to the mother to take her in at least for the summer was answered by telegram: "Impossible. Too awkward a situation for my husband. Stay in the college hall." The girl has had some glimmerings of what a different thing a Christ-centered life may be and is trying to do right, but if she succumbs to loneliness, heredity, and circumstances, is she the prodigal?

I met an American girl in Europe, exiled there in a school because of a mischievous act she committed which involved in an embarrassing situation sixteen persons who at some time, by way of numerous divorces and marriages, bore to her the relationship of parent or grandparent. As pagan as any Greek or Roman before Christ came, much more destitute of faith or training in virtue or righteousness than either Greek or Roman, she was held by no respect for law or God, but was just waiting for the freedom of twenty-one and complete control of her own fortune, unless she might perhaps meet some man whom she could "like well enough to stick it in marriage long enough to get free sooner." Church, religion, God, parenthood, duty, these were not even concepts to her. A young married woman in our Group held up a different ideal of marriage, of love, of life, to her, but as she had no time to carry through in their brief visit together, we can only hope and pray that the Word was sufficient to give her an ideal greater than that of her prodigal parents.

Divorce often brings to a child a separation from a loved parent and consigns him to the care of one toward whom he learns to feel resentment and rebellion because of that separation. That wise judges may have decreed it as just and fair does not remove the conflict and maladjustment resulting for the child. Have you ever considered the psychological consequences of the adjustments made necessary semiannually when a child has been assigned to each parent for half a year at a time? I've seen hundreds of such children and observed the character effects in later youth.

Frankie is illustrative of some of these effects. I've known him four years, from five to nine years of age. His mother and father were divorced for incompatibility, an alibi for rages, selfishness, and discourtesy, each equally guilty. Frankie still says, if suddenly or sharply rebuked: "Don't! don't! Mummy and Daddy talked like that and Mummy always cried."

At the beginning of each six months he has a difficult period of adjustment to new home conditions, new people, a new school. Then he is forced into defensive thinking and speaking of the absent parent, often without any provocation by the parent present, but as a part of his mental adjustment to an unwelcome change. Friends hear the mother say: "See how Frankie acts! The poor little lad is starved for love." And then the father: "That kid has come back completely spoiled. It will take six months to take the sullenness out of him." And frequently, both of them: "Thank God, Frankie will soon be old enough to be put into a good school where the teachers can make something out of him!"

Several girls of college age recently came to a house-party of the Oxford Group. They knew that they had been sent to the house-party to be "reformed," and they shared later their earlier amusement and conspiracy to defeat the "reformers" and to get some "larks" out of the trip. They found a supervision that was loving but complete, there was no "getting away with" escapades, drinking, or "petting parties." Inspired by the happy, care-free, frankly acknowledged Christian living and witnessing of the crowds of young people around them, they shared their desire for a changed life, their boredom, their secret shame.

Every one of these girls came from a broken home, divorced or separated parents!

But whatever the type of prodigal parent may be, the defect is the same. The thing lacking is the conscious, prayerful seeking for the guidance of God. Intelligence, love, and conscientious, honest intention may all be in the parent's attitude and procedure, and yet the youth may evidence the spiritual lack in the parent during his childhood. Error, and even sin, may arise in any human parent, but the answer, the way out, can always be found in honest sharing as guided by God.

CHAPTER VI

A FAMILY TALKS WITH GOD

ALMOST a year ago a happy young mother came unexpectedly to an Oxford Group meeting at Calvary[1] and told a story of the religious life of her children, to the accompaniment of much laughter but keen appreciation by her audience, of how God was being made real in that home. I asked for permission to use the story in this book, and her reply, by mail, merits full quotation and credit, for that home in Rochester is a joyful place where a whole family talks with God.

"It began two years ago, the actual talks, when I got up one morning and sat down with a pencil and paper and tried to formulate a program for a very busy day. Being a business woman, I had come to the point where I had to clear my mind before plunging into the hectic routine of the day, and as the early morning was my only free time, I had decided to try to use it as a preparation for the day.

"On this particular morning I was feeling very humble, as we had been through an unusual experience the night before. We had come home from a trip to find the children in a muddle about the question of 'babies

---

[1] Calvary is the name by which the Group people lovingly speak of Calvary P. E. Church, New York City, Rev. S. M. Shoemaker, Jr., rector.

and everything,' as they expressed it, and we had gone very thoroughly into every phase of it with them and had finally straightened it out satisfactorily. It was one of the times when we felt very close to one another because we had come close to a very deep and holy matter.

"When the time came for prayers we all knelt down together. It had occurred to us that if we said our prayers with the children we might get across the idea that prayers were not something to be gone through as a routine matter before going to bed, but that they were really experiences and brought people closer to God.

"Being an Episcopalian, it has always been hard for me to say a prayer in my own words. I had always felt that prayers in the Prayer Book were written by people who were trained to that and that I'd do well to stick to them, an attitude which I find was a quibble on my part. At any rate I, out of the fullness of my heart, said a prayer in my own words, and thanked God for my blessings. Whereupon the youngest boy, aged eight, said, 'Can I say my own prayer like that?' and proceeded to say this prayer: 'O God, thank you for giving me such a nice Mummie and Daddy and thank you for my nice brother and sister and I hope you will let us all get nice marks in school tomorrow and I hope that you know how much I love you. Amen, Peter.'

"Without any hesitation, Gina, the little girl, prayed, 'O God, thank you for letting Mummie tell us such a wonderful story about babies and everything and making it sound so nice when it sounded so horrid the way we talked about it in school.'

"And the older boy, Barclay, prayed, 'O God, help

me when I start out tomorrow in the new term to do my work with enthusiasm, to be the kind of boy so that all the boys will know what a wonderful Daddy I have.'

"By this time I was completely overcome, as it was the first time that we had ever done more than to say the regular prayers, 'Now I lay me down to sleep,' and asking God's blessing on our loved ones, and finally the Lord's Prayer. I was frankly dumfounded at the depth and the naturalness of the three prayers.

"So when I got up the next morning and tried to think through the day ahead, I had the feeling that I would have to do something about my life if I wanted to be in a position to keep pace with my children.

"I had not been at it long, in fact my thoughts had just begun to take shape in such commands as 'Don't get hectic,' 'Do one thing at a time,' 'Don't worry,' 'Take samples to Mr. F.,' 'Call painters about colors,' etc., when Peter came in and inquired what I was doing. I told him that I was thinking through my day, trying to plan things so that I wouldn't get confused and forget to do some important things. And he said, 'That's an awfully good idea. Wait a minute. I'll get my pencil and paper and be right with you.' So in he came, and with no hesitation sat down and began to write.

"Finally he said, 'How do you spell dishonest, Mummie?' I was rather startled and asked him why he wanted to know that. Whereupon he told me that God was trying to tell him something about being dishonest and he had to know how to spell it. I told him how, and when he got through he brought his paper to me and on it was written, 'Peter, if you will stop telling lies to your teacher and do your work right I will talk to you, but I don't like dishonest little boys.' I told him that I thought it was wonderful to have God talk to him like that, and said that I wished He would talk to me as clearly. Peter assured me that He would if I would listen.

"That was the first morning. Thereafter Peter and I used to listen every morning and one by one the other members of the family got interested. Before long all five of us were sitting with pencils and paper, listening for the commands for the day. It was very interesting to see the way each of us got a different kind of guidance. Peter still struggled with the lying. All of us had our particular faults brought to our attention, and always were shown a way to overcome them.

"Very shortly after we started, Peter suggested that we ought to have a book to write these things in, so that we could keep them. So I got five loose-leaf notebooks with our names on them, and as Peter said, 'We can keep these and when we are old we can look back and see if we have done what we were told to do.'

"During the years that we have been getting guidance, some wonderful things have happened. The problem of discipline has been simplified, as God is the disciplinarian for all of us. When a child tries to overcome telling lies because God doesn't like boys who lie, or when a girl is told to get her mother's help on the problem of telling dirty stories at school, when God tells a fourteen-year-old boy to help another boy at the risk of being laughed at by his friends and taunted as a sissy, and when the boy goes ahead knowing that God wouldn't tell him to do something impossible, and when God tells the boy to get his mother to help him get out of a mess he has gotten into through doing something dishonest in school, when these things are happening in a family, life is made much easier for parents. The problem of discipline is not only one of childhood. Parents often need it more than their children, as I have discovered for myself.

"It is a grand way to start the day—listening to God. There is nothing unnatural about sitting down with a pencil and writing down the thoughts that come to you. We have found that we have to check ourselves up. As one of the older children said, 'Sometimes we write down things because they sound well when we read them.' Sometimes I find that I write down things that I'd like to have God say to me but there is all the difference in the world between what comes straight and what doesn't. You can't pull the wool over your own eyes, and just as soon as we try to get away with make-believe our power is gone. The wonderful part of it is, the peace which comes with it. If God tells you to do something and you know that it is honest and unselfish, it doesn't matter what happens as a result of it. You can just put it off your mind and know that He will see that the outcome is right. So long as you are 'under orders,' you are confident that all is well. When you get rebellious and want to do things your way and run the show, then you are no good to yourself or anyone else. Then the thing that happens is, God says, as He did to our Peter, 'If you do what I tell you, and keep your thoughts from wandering, I will talk to you all the time; but if you don't, I won't talk to you any more.'

"It would be a sorry day in this family if God should stop talking to us, or if we should stop talking to Him. For when evening comes and we get down on our knees and listen to the children's prayers for us and hear them express their gratitude for the joys of the day just past and ask for strength for the day to come, all the petty, bothersome things seem to vanish and as a family we send up our thanks for God's talk with us and ours with Him."

A long distance away from this Rochester home lives another family that talks with God. It is a very different kind of a family, the most difficult kind of a family—a father, a wife, and four children of such varying ages that they often seem to add not one more generation, but two. In addition they usually seem to have one or more other persons living with them in the family. To bring all these varying points of view into one family focus seems, in the ordinary sense, almost impossible.

You will be interested in learning how they worked out their problem and I venture to quote from the father's letter to me.

"Our discoveries began to exceed our expectations when we began to teach religion to our first child. Until then we had not thought it necessary to have family prayers. When we did we stumbled along in conventional ways. Let us teach her the Lord's Prayer first, we said. But Margaret's mental processes did not at that time extend to the unseen and abstract. 'Our Father

—but you're my Daddy,' she said. 'Who art in heaven' involved a good deal of speculative theology. And when we came to 'Hallowed be Thy name' we gave up. The Lord's Prayer was the cornice, not the corner stone, of a prayer life.

"Then I suggested the beautiful prayers of the Church. But they were, at any rate, the top story. My wife urged spontaneous prayers from the heart. That was much better, but the vein of prayer soon ran out. It was then (for all this was early in the development of the Fellowship) that we thought of extending our own quiet time to the children. And at once we learned that to them it was a far more native element than it was even to us.

"I can remember well the second quiet time we ever had all together. Margaret was seven years old. We read a passage first, taking turns in the reading, and then the one who read asked questions of the others about the passage. This makes it a general enterprise, almost a game. Next follows a quiet time, and this is closed by a prayer and sharing all around. The whole lasts about half an hour. When it came Margaret's turn she looked straight up into my eyes and remarked, 'God told me Poppy should not raise his voice at Mamma.' For a second I may have been humiliated. Then I saw that here was a new relation of spiritual partnership coming into being. If I raised my voice it really was a family matter. I was glad, and not sorry, that she cared enough to face me with my own culpability. And to this day, without any loss of respect, we know we are partners, alike in our responsibility, under God, for our family life.

"We often begin our prayers at night with a quiet time. It makes the prayers themselves mean much more, because a real quiet time normally begins with convictions. On one such occasion I remember feeling that I could not begin until I shared that I realized that I had that morning 'raised my voice' as I shouldn't have, with her. 'Oh, that's all right!' she exclaimed. 'We all do those little things.'

"There is no trouble in harmonizing family relations if we go on this family principle. We know each other's errors and struggles, and we all feel equally interested. It makes us a family unit where age and occupations may separate. But above all, it makes us feel that God is a part of our family, very near, very holy and intimate. There is no unity but that which is founded in Him."

In Williamstown, Mass., the Hart family lives, their home being one of the places where I know a joyful welcome awaits me each summer. One of the boys, Sinclair, has already appeared in stories in this book. Marjorie, the mother, recently sent me some brief accounts of how two boys, one greatly handicapped from birth, may still learn to know God so that they can live on the basis of guidance and sharing. What a God-guided mother and father may do in developing the faith and character of children shines out so clearly in Marjorie's recital of these incidents that I use her words rather than my own. She writes:

"When my husband and I were having guidance to

go to Louisville with the team, I began to prepare the children for our being away for two weeks. The younger one, then eight and a half, was very loath to have us leave for so long and for such a distance. It meant having his quiet times alone, and having to get along without me to confide in, etc. Also, he is a bit of a worrier. Finally he said, 'What are you going to do there, Mummy?' I tried to explain that we were going because people there wanted us to tell them what we knew about Jesus. Immediately, with a lovely expression in his face, he answered. 'Why, then you are going to be missionaries; then I will let you go, Mummy.' I shared with him that I myself was a little afraid of my own shyness, and before we left, the whole family had a quiet time together. I know they prayed for us specifically while we were gone.

"This summer we had guidance that the time had come to send our elder boy to camp, and also the camp to which to send him became plain to us, too. He had never been away from us before, and because of a physical handicap, we knew it would be particularly difficult for him. So his father and I prayed that the child's own mind might be prepared for the ordeal. Two days before he was to go, after and during a terrific time of pre-homesickness, he shared, after our morning quiet time: 'God told me He would not let me be unhappy at camp.' The morning he left, he went off in high spirits, with a smile and a wave of the hand. All through that first bewildering week, I was told, he kept saying, 'I will be happy at camp.' He adapted himself unbelievably well, was happy, and even got through a case of measles away from home! He now wants to go again next year.

"A whole new system of being a parent is being developed in our family. Instead of that old trying method of keeping oneself on a pedestal to one's children, we try to make them feel that we are all the children of God, our Father, and we have quiet times together, when we pray for our individual needs, quite frankly, for one another, and for friends, and then have a 'listening time.' If God puts thoughts into our hearts and minds, we share them with one another, as guided, and it makes for a real feeling of understanding and helpfulness. It has been remarkable how it has helped them and me to live with a member of an older generation, who visits us over long periods, and I am often shamed by the loving patience exhibited by the younger boy. It far excels my own. When friction comes, we have a quiet time and pray for the offending person, and for patience and love for the rest.

"The value of honest sharing on the part of the parent is evident in this story. One morning recently it came to me to say in the family group, that I had been edgy the day before and was sorry. Immediately the younger boy, who had been very argumentative at breakfast, shared that he was sorry, too, and the day began better than it would have done otherwise.

"This fall a question arose as to which section it would be best for one boy to be in at school. We made it a matter of prayer as to whether I should speak to the school authorities again about it, and the boy himself got that it was best to just leave it to the teachers.

So we are honoring his guidance, and I am doing nothing more about it.

"To train the children in how to keep a quiet time by themselves, I compiled a short leaflet, which for a time they followed, but now they seem to prefer not to use the book. Quiet times with children must be short, and it is also, necessary when they get general and rather vague guidance like 'to be good,' or 'to be kind,' to make them think it through concretely, as to whom to be kind, and how.

"Our younger boy, when not more than six or seven, was very afraid of bad dreams. A doctor advised me to tell him that dreams are not real and that if he would remember that, when he was waked by them, he would not be scared. That was perfectly futile, and so we made up a game of saying 'abracadabra' to the dreams before he went to bed. That worked better, but I felt it was a wrong basis for the whole problem, so I prayed about it. The next morning the boy met me at his door, saying, 'I think God told me something. He told me to say abracadabra to Him as I do to Mother, and then He'll take the bad dreams away.' After that we had a special prayer about it before he went to sleep and he has had much better nights. When he does have dreams that frighten him, he is not so much upset by them."

Stories of the Twitchell children are so numerous in my collection that I hardly know which ones to relate. These are indeed inspired children, for they live in homes where the quiet time to seek and find (and follow!) God's guidance is the daily practice of the entire family of adults and children. Their summer home on

Long Island is a haven of peace to me, and the companionship of the children fills my life with amusement and interest as well as hope for their generation.

As I write, I can hear Skippy and Anne in their quiet time at night. In order to preserve a semblance of quiet, it was thought best recently to separate them, one having prayers with Marion, the mother, and the other with Madi, the governess, turn and turn about every other night. Sometimes, they accord me the high privilege of quiet time with both of them, Anne first and then Skippy.

A Bible story is told. I listen with carefully straight face as Anne tells that Jesus would not let them spend money on meat and things, bread and fishes were enough when He gave it out, and finishes up, as she always does finish her Bible story, *"C'est tout."* Or Skippy gives the story of the Prodigal Son, graphically describing colors and places, as he sees them familiarly around him, and the wickedness of the prodigal and how glad his father was to get him back. But never have I heard him mention the older brother in any telling of the story.

And then the singing in which we must all join. Shades of the family prayers of the past! What would those old patriarchs say to our songs at quiet time with Skippy and Anne? The last time I was there the repertoire included first, *"C'est un beau chateau,"* a French folk song that goes on forever like the "House that Jack Built." Then came "I think, when I read that sweet story of old," a new one just learned, which had to be repeated. Next was, "I've been working on the railroad," and finally, "Now the day is over," every stanza.

Down on our knees after that to listen to God and each of us to pray aloud in turn as the child chooses. The spontaneity of those prayers and their convicting sincerity and simplicity will be with me as long as I live.

Madi wrote me of one quiet time with Skippy when he was four years old. He had been willfully naughty at the supper table and she sent him to his room, depriving him of the hour's play between supper and bedtime. She was busy preparing his bath, when suddenly he ran to his bedside, saying, "I want to say prayers first tonight."

This was his prayer: "Dear Jesus, I was not good today. Help me to be a good boy all the time and I want to do the things when I am told and then we shall all be happy. You see, Jesus? Amen."

Listening to God in the quiet time solves all problems in the Twitchell families. Often the children's guidance carries the answer to the parents' problems. Last fall, Marian was not very strong and there was, furthermore, a new home adjustment to be made for the children. Yet there were several reasons why Marian should join her husband and work with the team then carrying the message of the Oxford Group to several places in Canada. All the family joined in a quiet time, children included, and through the children came the answer, "God says Mummy should go with Daddy to tell people about Jesus."

Billy's mother is one who feels deeply her duty towards the little boy whose life she is responsible for. Her own life is consecrated to God, her faith is a real and living one. She is a teacher of other children as well as mother of Billy. Although she lives a long distance away fom me, we have kept in touch with each other and I know her efforts to teach Billy to know God. I asked her to give me some stories showing how Billy had learned. She wrote me the following account, which I give entire, in her own words:

"I've always been formal in my own prayers and so I had to start there in teaching Billy. I never said nor liked 'Now I lay me.' Billy and I made up a little prayer of our own at first: 'Dear Father, take care of me and my Mamma and all the little children in the world this night, in Jesus name. Amen.'

"After I had tucked Billy into bed, I often would kneel beside his bed and repeat the Lord's Prayer and the Twenty-third Psalm. Then we both listened to what God had to say to us. Sometimes Billy was told to be a pleasant boy, sometimes he was sure God wanted Mamma to come to bed soon. A few times he was told to tell me about an unhappy experience of the day. Almost always his nurse had told me about it in private, but some few times it was my first information. The interesting part was he always assumed his full share of the blame or responsibility for the unpleasantness.

"He asked many questions about the 'Our Father.' With the help of the Holy Spirit, I was able to satisfy his desire for information. The Twenty-third Psalm seemed to go over more easily. I feel a little book called *The Wonder Book* helped him there. There are delightful poems and illustrations of David and his sheep, where they fed, drank, and rested, and a lovely poem of the first Christmas, and still another about the little children who went skipping and laughing on their way to see Jesus, and how he received them. The Psalm has been frequently a part of our prayer-time since. Billy has made some original contributions such as 'I shall not want for *anything*' and 'We shall dwell in God's house forever.'

"After sleeping for over two hours in Olive Jones' apartment one Sunday afternoon when I had an appointment with her, this was his contribution to our evening prayer: 'Father dear, please bless Mr. Shoemaker and all the folks who live in Olive Jones' house and keep them well.'

"Many times in my hurried and sometimes harried existence I have shown my exasperation in trying to deal with the natural problems that arise in a home. If I can just *stop* and bow my head or kneel down for a tiny quiet time, I always arise equal to the situation and Billy and I come to an understanding by Mom making an apology or Billy, often both, and then together we kneel and ask our Father to forgive us. Sometimes when Mother became too much of a problem for Billy, he bowed his head or would kneel down for a quiet time of his own. There was nothing that was more sure to make Mother see the error of her ways, and again we would ask God to forgive and help us to start anew.

"We do not limit our prayer life to unhappy or bedtime situations. We kneel down and thank Him for a particularly happy day, for a fine report from his nurse, for prompt recoveries from colds, for lovely gifts sent by loving friends.

"Two lovely experiences out of this past tragic winter of unemployment were Billy's prayer when he heard of little children who were cold and hungry: 'Father dear, please take care of the little children who are cold and hungry tonight. Tell the folks who need to have work done to get their Daddies to do it so there will be money to buy coal to build a fire." At both Christmas and Eastertime he offered to share his toys with less fortunate children. He insisted on giving his precious 'motorcycle cop' to a little boy in the Methodist Hospital in Brooklyn as his Church Christmas tree offering."

It is a truism to say that no influence is so potent in the spiritual, religious, and ethical life of a child as the prayers in babyhood with mother and father. Is your child's daily prayer-time your sacred and never-omitted joy and duty? Or are you waiting for his "intelligence to develop," an excuse so often given to me by parents, while servants are instilling fear or superstition?

CHAPTER VII

FINALLY, HOW?

THESE stories of "inspired children" have been told as a plea for spiritual freedom, joy, and naturalness in the religious life of children. They will have more than fulfilled their mission if they lead parents and teachers to seek and give simple and sincere sharing in their relationships with children, and to realize how ineffective and deadly in their ultimate influence on character may become the best pedagogic methods and equipment unless the vitality of true Christian faith and living is behind the teaching. It is a frequent saying in the Oxford Group that "You cannot give what you haven't got."

Hence the first requisite in discovering how to teach Christian qualities of character is an earnest and honest inquiry into your own spiritual condition. Do you listen daily for God's guidance? Can you face your world in regard to the standards of absolute honesty, absolute unselfishness, absolute purity, absolute love? Are you *willing* to remove any barrier by a complete surrender of yourself to God to "walk henceforth in His most holy ways"?

If you can answer these questions affirmatively, in so far as you know yourself in effort and intention, then you cannot go far wrong, for God will not only guide you directly, but He will lead you in your supplementary selection and study and use of the multitude of books on religious education produced since religion became a department of education. If you cannot, or more accurately will not, endeavor to incarnate for children and youth the faith and ideals you desire them to learn, do not be surprised when they throw them aside as unreal or antiquated.

The second requisite is to begin at the foundation itself. There is no use in building church membership and establishing creeds in the hope that they will teach and preserve character ideals or even religious faith. Sometimes they do, but never unless the solid foundation has been laid. Too often the pupil must in adult life tear down the walls and rebuild his foundations. This I know despite the fact that I love my church tremendously and have an unshakable credal belief.

What then is the foundation? Two elements enter into this foundation—prayer and study of the Bible. Prayer must be two-way prayer, asking and listening. The study of the Bible by very little children must include stories and memorizing.

The reasons for considering these elements to be the foundation of Christian character are obvious, but nevertheless I have ventured to give in Part Two of this book what I hope will prove to be useful and easily usable suggestions on how to build the foundation.

So far the discussion of "How" is intended for parents and teachers alike. There remain two more phases of the discussion. One is the later religious education of boys and girls after the foundation is laid.

I mention it merely to show that it is not forgotten, but it is beyond the purpose of this present volume.

The second is how can a church school carry on religious education so as to achieve greater permanency of spiritual influence than seems to be apparent among young people today? I might give you a dissertation on this subject which you would probably discard as "deadly dull" or "old stuff," because I do not know how to express in the language of pedagogy or psychology a thing so subtle. So I tell you the story of how one church school is doing it, praying, as I write, that God will drive home to every teacher who reads it an aspiration to fit the story into his own church or class conditions.

To begin with, in our church school we had an understanding rector. He knew little about education, maybe less about children, but he did know Jesus Christ and he was living a guided life. He knew that boys and girls cannot learn to love and follow Jesus Christ when Sunday-school attendance is hated and forced; when teachers fail in regular attendance, in preparation of the lesson, and in any sense of responsibility for tracing the effect of their teaching; when tumultuous disorder prevails even during the worship service; when the curriculum is unsuitable in grading and content; in short, when the work has neither aim nor functioning power and is merely one more organization in an institutional church.

Some of his advisers urged him to close the school, but his own guidance was to wait and to study the situation, knowing that God would show the way children, the church of the future, could be adequately cared for. It is important to note that he waited for God to show the way. I have known many ministers, facing similar conditions in a church school, who have sought aid from colleges of education and obtained excellent results, judged by pedagogic standards. But what about the spiritual significance of the work as shown in changed lives? "You cannot give what you haven't got," as the Group says. Hence, there must be a surrendered, guided will, a changed life, in minister and superintendent and director of religious education, if the message of Christ is to carry over into living faith and action in adult life.

When the school closed in late May or early June of 1928, the rector, Mr. Shoemaker, announced to the entire church membership that there would be a complete reorganization of the church school in the fall. He also stressed the importance of a church school, and some of our own school needs in particular. He closed his announcement with an invitation, open to anyone in the entire congregation at all interested in the religious education of children, to attend a series of conferences to be held on Monday evenings throughout the month of June for discussion and guidance concerning standards, curriculum, and the selection of a staff of teachers. I was asked to lead these conferences.

About fifty men and women responded, including all of the clergy. Many of the former staff of teachers eliminated themselves by failure to attend these conferences. Out of those conferences came, under God's guidance, four ideas, noteworthy changes in the procedure of building a church school, although we did not realize that at the time.

The first was the staff of teachers, for their names came in answer to prayer as clearly as the words on this page appear to your eye now. They were not selected for knowledge of methods of education. Only two or three had any, but they were all willing to learn and they readily applied the suggestions given. They were not even all selected because they "belonged to the Group" or because they had given any signal witness as to changed lives, but they were all truly seeking to know God and were unashamed in the acknowledgment of their faith, this at a time when religious conversation was socially taboo. All but two of that first staff of teachers have come into a vital experience of Christ and most of them are active workers in one or more of the Oxford Groups today. Just why they were selected and how they became a team will become clear later. No vacancy has ever been filled except with a teacher who has made a genuine surrender to Christ.

The second idea was to have two teachers in each class. At first this plan met with some difficulty, due chiefly to the self-consciousness of teachers about teaching under the observation of another person, but to some extent also to my own lack of consideration of differences in temperament, age, or experience of teachers placed together. Both difficulties were solved through frank sharing at the teachers' meetings, and the plan itself has solved many of the most frequent and annoying difficulties which occur in a church school. The substitution of an unprepared teacher, a stranger to the children in a class, when a teacher is absent, does not exist among us. Yet at the same time there is no heavy burden of obligatory attendance placed upon a teacher when an emergency or something of personal importance arises, provided he notifies the other teacher who shares a class with him. The disturbance of children's attention and the interruption to the teacher's thought caused by the entrance of a visitor or a secretary are prevented because one teacher, not at the moment engaged in instruction, is free to care for inquiries, collections, and records.

The third idea was an advisory council of adult members of the church from whom to draw future teachers and through whom we kept interest in the church school alive among the older people, not parents or teachers, and secured financial support, as well as approval of apparently revolutionary plans. This council did noble service for us, especially its very devoted chairman, Miss Louise Warren. The council also constituted our first Adult Bible Class. Miss Eugenia Boross, now Mrs. John Cuyler, did an unforgettable piece of work in this class. She taught its members not only to know a Bible lesson, but how to study it. She not only pointed out its applications to their lives, but she followed them up to win, through personal interview and honest sharing, their own acceptance of the lesson and God's guidance. Out of that council class came some of our best teachers in later days.

The fourth idea was that curriculum, equipment, and method are of far less importance than leading children to know and feel the power of the Holy Spirit as motivation for the ideals and standards we want to inculcate. You may have lime and clay, you may even heat and grind them together in huge cylinders, but until you have added water, you have no cement for your hard concrete foundation. "Except the Lord build the house, they labor in vain that build it." Therefore, although we had a curriculum from the very first and strove valiantly to obtain and equip class-rooms, our major emphasis was and is on the quiet time, concerning which you will read in Chapter X, we having all agreed at our teachers' meetings that prayer is the beginning of all knowledge of God.

The one great instrument we worked with was our teachers' meetings. We have never used outside inducements to secure the attendance of teachers. We have never permitted the teachers' meetings to be used for announcements, records, fault-finding, planning campaigns for money, or any other dry detail of administration. God is the only speaker invited, and we listen to His voice first at every meeting and share what comes, honestly and good-naturedly, whether praise or criticism be implied. Sometimes, as a teacher shares guidance at the close of a quiet time, we hear him say to the secretary, aloud so that his associates hear: "I'm sorry for the mistakes in my records. It came to me that they are very careless and must make hard work for you. I'll do better." Or sometimes to me, "I haven't prepared my lessons very well lately and the work has suffered. I'm sorry. Will you show me how to make it up to the children?"

Our curriculum content and our methods of instruc-

tion have been shaped or modified by the guidance of
the teachers' quiet times together. Valuable and valid
have been the suggestions thus obtained. Some of the
guidance read at our teachers' meetings will linger with
me always. I hear them now say:

"I can't make my children interested in the lessons
we're having now. Can some one show me what I'm doing wrong?"

Everybody would join in the ensuing discussion.
There are no laws of curriculum or method which cannot be broken, amended, or discarded, if the guidance
after a final quiet time agrees that the lessons are unsuitable or the instructions are inadequate. No one dic-
tates commands and no one is offended, not even the
superintendent who wrote the criticized instructions.
Nor is the teacher if the resultant agreement is that he
is in error or has misunderstood, even if he is met by
hearty laughter, as often happens.

Sometimes a teacher shares a personal matter and we
set aside every other question to rejoice or to sorrow
or to aid, always to pray. We all remember the day
when Phyllis and Burke told us it was their last term
in our church school and that they were going to build
a school together in another city. Their joyful looks
were ours too, and the bond among us was tightened
because we shared in their joy. What a time we did
have, many times, in fact, over the engagements and
marriages in that first group of teachers! And what a
feeling of partnership we have in the religious education
of the babies as they come along, praying in full faith
that God will guide the parents to use and develop

further the methods we worked out together! When our secretary, Sarah Elizabeth Gustam, went down South to be director of religious education in a church school, we all felt that she was our missionary and laid aside all other questions to pray for her guidance.

When one of our young men told, in a quiet time at one of our teacher's meetings, that he could not teach the Old Testament because he doubted its truth, we found ourselves divided into many thought-groups ranging all the way from extreme fundamentalism to modern Biblical criticism. But honest talk, loving sharing, and God's guidance gave us a common ground on which we could stand in our teaching. When one of the younger women teachers said that she "couldn't get any guidance" and that she thought "God did not want her to teach children, she wasn't good enough," we had a long time of prayer, and then two or three slipped off with her to talk alone, this having been their guidance in that time of quiet and prayer.

Nor need there ever be any fear that this type of personal, intimate sharing will spoil the efficiency of any teacher or divert attention from the major reason for teachers' meetings, the consideration of the interests of the children in the church school. Providing always that we ourselves as a staff of teachers keep ourselves individually open to the guidance of God, a corps of teachers listening to the voice of God in the quiet time of their teachers' meetings will be united in purpose and ideals, a working team.

PART TWO

The Way
How Children Learn to Know God

CHAPTER VIII

SOME POINTS OF VIEW ON RELIGIOUS EDUCATION

THE material presented in the stories of this book might very aptly be called notes from practical experience in the religious education of children, for most of it is the outcome of actual work in a church school, both Sunday and week-day sessions. But the writer, or rather the compiler of this material, has certain other purposes in view besides suggestions to teachers and parents.

The first purpose is to show that spiritual reality is possible for children. Unless it begins in childhood, it is learned and obtained only through suffering and struggle. A second is to find the way, not necessarily to refute, but certainly to prevent for the future, any truth in the assertion that religious education has no effect in shaping character and in preventing criminality.

A third purpose, just as needed even if temporarily more limited in scope, is to show parents and teachers, who have recently come into a more vivid and further-reaching experience of Christ themselves, how to pass that new spiritual light on to children and youth, so that it will become a guiding power outlasting the teacher and holding more securely in ways of right living than either ethical instruction or habit-training has yet shown power to do. Some of us in the past ten years or so have come to believe that there are certain fixed and fundamental principles which underly that power and are conditional to such a spiritual experience. We believe that even little children can learn and understand these principles and can apply them in their childish problems.

These are great aims, possibly too ambitious for realization in any one book or by any one person. Several incidents of recent occurrence have prompted the desire to hold these aims before us. One is the publication of a research into the ethical judgments of some thousand young people and the relation of these judgments or character analyses to religious education, including, apparently, a conclusion that there is no proof of any relationship between the two, or rather that religious training does not bring about a right ethical decision.

Another is the publication of a research into the previous religious experience of the inmates of a great prison, apparently demonstrating that 90 per cent of these offenders against the law had had religious instruction which had utterly failed to influence their lives. A third is the urgent utterance of some leaders in pre-school education against teaching religious ideas to children as being introspective, leading to self-consciousness, and "emotionally repressive," whatever that may be, or as arousing fear and false notions of life and science resulting in "conflicts" and "complexes" when contradictions are discovered.

Still another is the type of religious education which has been too general during the past ten or fifteen years. It has lacked vitality and has failed to give reality of spiritual experience. It has only been another subject added to the curriculum. Boys and girls have learned about the Bible, about the church, about God, as they learned a science or the history of Rome or the life of Lincoln, and the same destructive criticism has entered into all of it. The same faint praise has damned the story of Christ as it has the life of Washington. The same mistakenly conceived "scientific attitude" has entered into the study of the experiences of the spirit as into our observation of material things and substances.

These are assaults upon the very basis of character. And their own foundation is untruth, their assertions and assumptions cannot stand the light of reality, of truth, of our deepest, if secret, experiences. They rely upon our accepting the assumptions or upon our heated controversial attempts at refutation. Our hope is to do neither, but to build constructively, by means of practical aids to teachers and mothers especially, so that the assertions, if true today, need no longer continue to be facts, and so that the spiritual reality in the religion of the youth of tomorrow may be the truest refutation because it is demonstrable fact and not controversial utterance.

This brings us to a consideration of what is the beginning of spiritual experience. How does a child get his first ideas of God, of religion, of things of the spirit? Are they always taught by some one? Are they merely the results of home or school or social environment? Or are they God-given, born with us and within us, as certain to grow and be developed by the influences around us, for good or evil, as any emotion or aptitude or talent grows or dies, is expressed or controlled?

Recently a child of ten or eleven came to us, brought by a puzzled mother. She was an only child, born of parents of opposing and irreconcilable faiths who had agreed that neither would teach the child any religious creed, but would permit her at the proper (?) time to become acquainted with all creeds and choose her own. Somewhere, somehow, prompted so far as any one can learn or she herself can tell, by God alone, that child got the idea of praying to God. She could not tell what she meant by God and she evidently had never thought of either His personality or His habitation. Her chief prayer was that God would "make Mamma and Papa stop fighting," and later that God would "make Papa let her go" to a children's club in a church attended by some playmates. Neither parent had refused permission, neither knew she wanted to go. But there was no religion in her home, neither went to any church so far as she knew, although both did observe alone the essential holy days of their respective faiths, secretly so far as the child was concerned, and she had received an association of fear in relation to any mention of church. God was taboo in her home!

The child's prayers and her troubled thinking about the whole question became known to the mother finally through her questioning into various conditions which arose with the child. The father was unsympathetic, inclined to pooh-pooh the seriousness of the issue in the child's mind, and accused the mother of violating her agreement about the child's religious training, in spite of the fact that the church the child was drawn to belonged to the creed of neither father nor mother, but was equally irreconcilable to either one. It is an unfinished story, as we have known the child only a few months, but the story points my question, illustrates my belief that the cry for God and for spiritual reality is a part of our very being as much as seeing or feeling, and that that cry is fulfilled or denied in just so far as we permit the forces of evil to prevail against it.

Hence my profound appeal for better thinking about religious education. It may be very much more dramatic to convert a drunkard and see him rebuild his life, but why let him get so low? It may be much more thrilling to change the life of a débutante and send her out to use her talents in converting others to Christ, but why let her grow up without knowing Christ? We are spending heaps of money and using the lives of noble, consecrated men and women in rescue-mission work and in evangelistic fields, but we are doing almost nothing to reach children and start them right.

It is true that there is little drama or thrill in religious education. Much of it is grinding repetition, again and again, day after day. And for most of it one never has the chance of seeing results or of knowing whether either drama or thrill will ever eventuate, for the children pass out of our lives through the changes time brings or death takes us out of their lives. My work for little children is one of faith and hope and brings me no sense of finished achievement or even of certainty for the future of any child, and there is practically nothing in it that can bring great worldly prestige, let alone drama or thrill or acclaim for a recognized, finished performance.

Hence, too, my belief in prayer. And out of my reliance upon prayer in my work for children has come my realization of the fact that in prayer, in making prayer real to children, comes the beginning of their religious thinking and should come the beginning of religious education, not in any teaching of creed or even of the Bible or of ideas of God. To the place of prayer in the religious education of children we give our first attention.

CHAPTER IX

REAL PRAYERS FOR CHILDREN

OUR age is interested in the beginnings of things, what makes them happen, whether they are real or make-believe. We are searching for reasons and explanations, whether it be of wave-lengths or neurasthenics, a bank failure or a theological student, a Ghandi or a Mussolini. We have come into a new period whose shibboleth is research and whose panacea is the questionnaire. It is about time that some one began to analyze the returns in a way which will give concrete, helpful, practically usable answers to the problems exposed by the questionnaire, instead of leaving parents and teachers discouraged, doubting, and neglectful, and children untrained in the way which would help them escape the difficulties and sins inevitably consequent upon neglect, ignorance, and lack of established habits. It is to give a few practical suggestions on one of the problems so revealed that this chapter on prayer is written.

Character and religious education have not escaped the research method. First and foremost in the problems made conscious to us all through research studies of the prayer life of children and of adults is how to teach children to pray and to keep reality in their thought of prayer and of God. It is a basic problem, its solution is essential for character-training.

Without righteousness there is no stability to character. Without religion there is no sure and lasting reason for righteousness. Without prayer there can be no reality to religion. Hence prayer is the very beginning of religious education, and religious education should begin when the child's power to speak begins, even sooner. As soon as the child can understand words, he is old enough to learn the attitude of prayer. The thought, the meaning of prayer, he grasps from his parents' attitude and from their words of prayer. God forgive the parents if they lack reality in prayer in the presence of a little child!

So let him kneel or bow the head when father or mother prays, and let him call it prayer. Let him become accustomed to hearing the use of the words, "pray," "prayer," "bow," "kneel," "God." Then when he can talk ever so little, let him begin to pray his own prayers, not to *say* prayers, but to *pray*. Teaching him to say, "Now I lay me" or other prayers of the unreal, old-time childhood tradition makes for unreality in the prayer life of children of today. Compare those rhyming prayers, said to the unlistening ears of a modern nurse, with the scientific toys which the same child plays with! Which is real and which is bathos?

His first prayers must be a natural self-expression. Remember the child has been thinking long before he speaks. If his prayer is to be a real expression of himself to God and is to lead to a real discovery of his real relationship to God, it must be an expression of himself in his own self-chosen words. The instinctive self-expression of the child is selfish; he is concerned and interested in his own body, his own movements, his own needs. Reality for him begins with them and his first prayer will be instinctively about his own desires and needs. Do not check or laugh at those baby prayers, but use the opportunity of the prayer-time to develop the unselfish idea and lead his prayer thought, and resultantly his social thought, from the selfish to the unselfish. This first prayer, whether selfish or unselfish, if it is a natural self-expression, will almost surely be petition.

As soon as he can grasp the thought at all, teach him to add the idea of thanksgiving to his prayer. Avoid making it formal. Develop the thought of thanksgiving in prayer in exactly the same way as you develop with the child the idea of saying "thank you" for something received. Make it just as simple and natural, and impress it by repetition, as the mother does with the baby's "ta ta." The next step to be added to the child's prayer thought is that of intercession. Make it equally natural self-expression—for a playmate, for some one who is sick or unhappy. A little child in our church school recently prayed for God to make Papa smile. A whole sermon on the relation of father to child lies in that prayer.

Finally the thought of worship must become a part of the child's prayer. Again emphasis must be laid upon its being developed so that it is a natural self-expression and not an imposition of an adult idea.

Let me urge that teacher and parent keep away from

any definition of God or any limitation of His personality by human comparisons. Reasons for this recommendation will appear later. The prayer of worship carries with it the recognition of God. Let it be the child's own conception of God, influenced only by the ideas of goodness and love, necessarily drawn from the teaching of prayer already indicated.

When the child's prayer includes worship, he has begun to make God real in his life, something more than another man or another parent, but, however faintly, however childishly, nevertheless God, the great Father of all.

The progression in this natural self-expressive prayer, then, is from the selfish to the unselfish, and it is inclusive of first petition, next thanksgiving, next intercession, and finally worship. It is impossible to say at what age a child will grasp these various prayer thoughts. It is probable, possibly even desirable, that they should not be too consciously or explicitly grasped by children at a very early age, but it is desirable that the habit of such prayer thought, and the *feeling* of it, should be implanted early.

The prayer of self-expression, in children's own words, is the beginning of the prayer thought, but there should soon be added the use of certain set or stated or formal prayers. The addition of the formal prayer may help in the development of the progression of prayer thought just outlined, but the parent and the teacher must be careful not to destroy the child's naturalness and unself-consciousness when the formal prayer is taught.

At the same time there are several reasons why we should teach children to say certain set or stated prayers. In the first place, they provide models of what prayer should really be. Children are inevitably led to imitate these prayers, just as they will imitate the prayer of father or mother if said aloud before them. In the second place, the idea of unity in prayer is impressed, if children are led to say a formal prayer aloud in unison with other children or with parent or teacher. It is easy to lead children to see that if they are all to pray for the same thing they must pray in the same words, or else confusion and discord result instead of unity. In the third place, the teaching of a formal prayer leads to reverence in attitude and speech and thinking. Just as we adults instinctively use a different tone of voice in the repetition of the formal Prayer Book prayer from the tone used in our informal, self-expressive prayers, so does the child. This can be used to help him grasp the idea of and the reason for reverence. It makes a good introduction to the inclusion of worship as a part of his own self-chosen words of prayer.

This teaching of the formal prayer should begin just as soon as parent or teacher feels that the child has progressed far enough in his prayer thoughts, and from that time on there should proceed side by side the formal prayer and the self-expressive prayer. The formal prayer to be said in certain set and stated phrases taught to the child must be carefully chosen. It should not be above his comprehension. It should be simple in language. At first it should include only those steps in prayer progress which he has already begun to use in his informal, self-worded prayer. Finally the formal prayers must include all the steps in prayer thought which have already been outlined for the prayer of self-chosen words.

About this time in the child's prayer life the use of the Lord's Prayer should be introduced, and it should be memorized and later said repeatedly as a whole. It is the only perfect model of a prayer ever written. The teaching of it, portion by portion, may be begun long before its use as prayer and not necessarily as a part of the child's prayer-time. It should be taught a phrase at a time as listed below, each new phrase being carefully joined to the preceding one.

Our Father—Who art in Heaven—Hallowed—Be Thy Name.—Thy Kingdom come—Thy will be done —On Earth—As it is in Heaven.—Give us this day our daily bread—And forgive us our trespasses—As we forgive—Them that trespass against us;—And lead us not into temptation,—But deliver us from evil;—For Thine is the Kingdom—The Power—and the Glory —Forever and ever—Amen. It may be taught as part of Scripture lessons. It may be taught as memory work. It should be taught through picture and illustration. Every modern aid to the teaching of memory gems in literature should be included, so that the Lord's Prayer will not be taught as mere words or a jingle or a hated exercise. There are scores of suggestions available for such a teaching of the Lord's Prayer, which can be obtained from houses which publish Sunday-school aids.

After the Lord's Prayer has been learned and as children are approaching the age of confirmation or membership in the church, other prayers of the church should be used as the model formal prayers to be used in conjunction with their self-worded prayers. I especially recommend in this respect the prayer known as A General Thanksgiving in our Episcopal Church service of Morning Prayer and many of the Collects of the Book of Common Prayer.

Now for some detailed suggestions in regard to the conduct of prayer-time, whether at home by parents or in school by the teacher. Children should say their prayers sometimes aloud and sometimes silently. The silent prayer must be encouraged in order to give the child the idea of communion with God and of freedom of approach to God. The prayer said aloud gives the feeling of unity with others in prayer. It destroys self-consciousness and makes the prayer-time natural. It provides to the parent and to the teacher the opportunity to note correctness of impression and of expression and the progress the child has made in his prayer thought.

Again children must be taught lovingly and naturally to pray alone and also with others. There is an absolute naturalness in both of these for children, unless the parent or the teacher interjects the unnatural or the self-conscious idea. This was recently illustrated by a child in our church school who had learned from her teacher to have a "quiet time" for praying to God and listening to God. One night she called in an adult relative and said, "Don't you think you ought to have a quiet time with God? Wouldn't you like to have a quiet time with me and both of us listen to God?"

The attitude of prayer is important. Children get it earliest by following our example, but they should learn to recognize it and to use it appropriately. They should learn why we bow our heads or kneel or stand in prayer. They should learn when these attitudes of prayer are used. They should learn to know that we close our eyes in prayer in order to shut out the distractions of things about us and commune with God without interruption. Learning by example and imitation the attitude of prayer, they come naturally to an appreciation of the atmosphere of prayer. Every effort should be made by parent and teacher to establish and preserve the atmosphere of prayer, both to secure reality and to instil reverence. The instilling of reverence for God through the attitude of prayer and preserving the atmosphere of prayer will be one of the best preventives to profanity and foul language that either parent or teacher can use. The boy or girl to whom God is real, who has learned reality in prayer, and who associates the name of Jesus Christ with prayer, cannot be led astray by the language which is so painfully common among girls as well as boys.

In our church school we have been trying to put some of these ideas concerning prayer into practice during the past four years, and we feel great gratitude and encouragement from some of the observations we are making of the way children are applying their teaching. To begin with, in sessions where the whole school assembles, we taught them to kneel and bow their heads when they enter the church for the worship service which precedes the lesson. Next we led them to see and to tell the reason for this action. Then we led them to tell us what should be included in the prayer that they say at that moment. The three things which we have learned from them so far are that we ask God to bless our church school, that we ask God to help the teachers teach the lesson well, that we ask God to help the pupils listen and learn the lesson. So far, of course, this expressed prayer is petition and partly intercession. We have still to take the other steps of thanksgiving and worship. We have made no effort yet to teach any formal prayer for use as a prayer upon entrance, except that occasionally I remind the children of the three things which they have told me we should ask God for in that opening prayer.

The unconscious irony to be found in one small lad's prayer makes a story too good to withhold. He always sat in the end of the very front seat and always said his opening prayer aloud, his head bowed and hands firmly held over closed eyes. As the other children paid no attention to his voice, we never disturbed him, not wishing to induce self-consciousness or fear. But I often wondered how an ill-prepared teacher felt when his voice boomed out, "God bless our school. God make the teachers learn the lesson right. God make us listen."

Another prayer lesson which we have taught looks towards the idea of unity and will be an introduction to formal prayer. This step consists in the teaching of the word "amen." The children told me that saying "amen" after a prayer is finished means that we agree with the prayer. We used this idea to develop the thought that if they are going to say "amen," they must mean they agree, and therefore they must listen to what they say they agree to.

Much further development in prayer thought and prayer time has been made by individual teachers in the class lesson period. With some of the older children, both boys and girls, the idea of the quiet time has been well developed. Children pray aloud and they pray silently and they pray in unison with their teachers. They tell to one another the thoughts that God gives them during their quiet time after their silent prayer. The influence is far-reaching and incalculable.

Often teachers sincerely desiring to give to their children reality and reverence in prayer are puzzled in regard to the best method of approach to the subject and hamper their accomplishment by errors of detail, by digressions, by distractions to attention, even by harsh commands and other mistaken attempts at discipline. A few suggestions from the experience of practical and successful teachers may be useful to show how, in a class-room with a group of children, a teacher may lead children to a real prayer-time, just as surely as a mother with an individual child or a leader of adult Christians. These suggestions will be found in Chapter XI.

Let me close this chapter as I began it. Religious education begins when the child begins to speak. His religious thinking may begin before that. Teaching him to pray is the first step in his religious education. Without reality in prayer his religion will never be vital.

CHAPTER X

THE QUIET TIME

IN AN earlier chapter reference was made to certain fundamental principles which are conditional to a vital spiritual experience and to our belief that even little children can learn and understand and apply these to their childish problems, thus establishing habits of thought and action which will continue and control in later life. These principles are not new. They are as old as the Gospels themselves. Christ taught them. The Epistles of Paul, Peter, James, and John explain and emphasize them. They have been frequently re-stated down through the centuries by consecrated and inspired workers for Christ in terms and phrases suitable to their times and peoples.

In the Fellowship, in our turn, we have come to use certain words as expressing these principles briefly and pertinently. I shall not attempt here a discussion of these principles, either their truth or their definition, but I give you briefly the terms we use which embody the principles which children do grasp and practice, although we attempt no terminology with them nor do we advise it.

Conviction, by which we come to a conscious realization of our sins which shut God away from us.

Confession, which leads us to make an honest statement of our wrong-doing to God and to the human against whom the wrong act was committed.

Restitution, by which we make amends, restore, so far as human power permits, for the wrong done.

Conversion, which means simply a changed life. "Ye must be born again," said Christ.

Sharing, by which we enter into fellowship with all those who have sought and found God or are seeking and learning to know Him.

Surrender, by which we gratefully give to God in reverent worship and pledged devotion our will, that gift which He gave to us with full freedom to use for good or evil, and with our will we yield every desire, thought, and act not in accordance with His great plan for us.

Guidance, the voice of God speaking to us in direction of our lives, coming to us in the quiet time as we pray to God with barriers removed and will surrendered to do His bidding.

I do not propose or believe that children use and understand these terms. They are stated here as principles. They are basic facts and acts without which a spiritual experience can neither begin nor continue. They give reality and reason to existence itself. But that children grasp these principles, apply them, and express them, we do contend and can prove.

Nay more, in the truth of this contention lies the solution of the three great purposes this book set out to accomplish. In the acceptance of this truth lies the power of parent and teacher to set a child's feet in the pathway toward God and righteous living. In a generation thus taught, thus brought into conscious relationship with God, shall the world find the answer to the issues which harass men's souls today.

The practical question before us, then, is: How is it done? What is the method of approach? What is the teaching technique by which children do grasp these principles understandingly? There is no mystery. There is no "pedaguese." The approach to God is always through prayer, and the child comes into comprehension of the way to God in the quiet time by the direct teaching of God Himself, when parent or teacher gives but just the unspoiled opportunity. Hence the emphasis on prayer in the previous chapters, and hence the suggestions which follow about how to conduct a quiet time and how to lead children to continue the practice of quiet time when alone.

There should be very little specific instruction other than the teaching to pray described in the previous chapter. The best way to learn how to have a quiet time is to have one. I quote now from the answer to this question given by a young teacher in our church school, afterward adopted as a general recommendation to all teachers in the school:

"Children enter the class-room talking with one another and greeting the teachers. Outdoor clothing must be removed and disposed of safely and neatly, and news must be exchanged if attention is to be more than a surface thing later. Two, or at most five, minutes only must be allowed for greetings and removal of clothing. Teacher then suggests in a cheerful and friendly tone and manner, 'Let us ask God to guide us in today's lesson. Maybe God will tell us something to share with one another.' A period of absolute silence should follow, children and teachers seated. The length of the period will vary from one to ten minutes, according to the age and grade of the children. Even with the oldest children the length of this quiet time should rarely exceed five minutes. With the young children it should rarely exceed two minutes. *But note,* no hard and fast rule can be set for the length of the quiet time for children any more than for adults. Much depends upon their grasp of religious thinking and upon the teacher's spirituality.

"The quiet time should be ended by prayer. As confidence and spiritual feeling grow, children themselves can and will make prayers themselves. Teachers should encourage them to do so. Following the prayers, opportunity should be provided for sharing the thoughts, the directions received, during the quiet time. Teachers should share with their children."

Sincerely and naturally conducted, the quiet time is the teacher's most precious instrument in the major aim of Sunday-school teaching, namely that children may find God early in life and learn to recognize His voice, whether in conviction or in guidance. It may become the teacher's own means of spiritual growth as he or she learns from the simplicity and directness of childhood. It is the most characteristic and significant feature or our church-school work, but it must be real and not perfunctory, sincere and not formal religious ceremony. Else it fails in its beneficent and spiritual values and we lose the approach to God it might afford us.

It is in the sharing that the teacher or parent discovers how God is leading a child spiritually and finds his or her own opportunity to correct errors, to give lasting reality to the child's experience, and to make known to the child through his own conscious expression the principles of Christian living he has found out by prayer and experience.

CHAPTER XI

As Two Teachers Tell It

1. A Teacher of Older Girls

THE following material was used once for an address by the teacher who wrote it, who is still teaching in our church school. It serves admirably as a restatement and a new emphasis on the thoughts presented in the preceding chapters on how to make God and religion vitally molding factors in a child's training. She called her address

MAKING CHRIST REAL TO CHILDREN[1]

Children receive their first religious experiences at second hand, at first from their parent and the home, and later from their church-school teachers or perhaps in day school. This is what makes necessary the existence of a real religious experience in the adult who attempts to make God real to the child. I cannot emphasize too strongly the fact that the prime requisite of any teacher of religion is that the teacher have a genuine experience of Christ and that it be a live and growing one. Children are interested in a religious

[1] The writer is now Mrs. Burke Rivers, wife of a clergyman in New Haven. She taught the highest grade in Calvary Church School for three years.

"once upon a time" story, but they are captivated by a story of what God has done in the teacher's own life. They sense the freshness of it and are eager to enter into such an experience themselves. It is well to remember that children are frequently more clear visioned than their elders, and are not fooled by any pretentious mask of knowledge of God that the teacher may assume before them.

Since the whole aim of the teacher is that the child may come to know God as an intimate reality, it is necessary for the teacher to believe that the experience of God which he possesses can be transferred to the child; in other words, that the child can have as genuine a religious experience as can the teacher. This does not mean that the child is thought of or treated as an adult, but it should be kept in mind that Christ loved the little children and bade them come unto him.

This brings us naturally to the question of how the teacher shall approach the child. We hear much of the parent "coming down" to the child's level, or of treating the child as an equal, which means, I suppose, as an adult. From my own contact with children I have learned that there is a common level of honesty and confidence on which we can meet. On the teacher's part, this implies love for the child and also approachability. It is sometimes easier to love the child than to feel at home with him and his problems.

It is a good thing for the teacher to live through again in memory his life as a child. Soon enough it is discovered how much has been forgotten, but this is an invaluable exercise if he is wholly to appreciate the child's life and problems. They center largely around the home, the school, and the social life, as well as in the inner thought life of the child. Such factors as family background, especially the relationship of the boy or girl with the parents and brothers and sisters, the school enthusiasms and difficulties, fears, dislikes, and ambitions, all enter into the picture. If we are to help the child we must have an intimate knowledge of the content of his life.

All this brings us to the threshold of the actual business. *How* does the child come to know God personally? What does "surrender" to God's will involve for him? How should the subject of sin be dealt with? Summed up the question is, How does the process whereby the teacher came to know God work for the child?

It has never been necessary to give the children whom I have taught a definition or description of sin in order for them to recognize it, nor have I attempted to give them a conviction of sin. It is a rare adult group of whom this can be said. Children have an uncanny way of knowing what is wrong in themselves as well as in us. They are extraordinarily honest, as a rule, in dealing with it, provided they are not frightened. Again and again it has come about that in the time of quiet listening to God conviction has come to the child. It may be a matter of getting up earlier in order to be at school on time, or of being disciplined in the spending of an allowance, or the conviction may be one of selfishness in not wanting to take care of a baby sister. During the time of sharing there is an opportunity for all these things to come out and the teacher has the chance to help in the process of restoration.

It is necessary to make it clear that these sins of petty dishonesty, fear, quarreling and disobedience are what keep them from the whole experience of God, and then to tell them simply, and from one's own personal knowledge, that they must first make things right and then that Jesus Christ can take these sins away if they will let him.

Some people wonder whether this is morbid. Let me tell you about two nine-year-old girls who quarreled almost every time they played together. Each one would go home and tell her mother that never again would she play with the other one. Of course they soon forgot the solemn vow and played and quarreled with the same result. One Sunday in the class quiet time one girl shared with us, the other girl being present, that God had told her it was wrong for her to always scrap with Helen. Immediately Helen responded, and there in the class-room we talked it over and laughed about it. Finally the girls made a decision themselves that it was a foolish way for them to act and they wouldn't do it any more. I haven't heard of any quarrels since. It was a healthy settlement of the problem of getting along with one's neighbor, which is not always confined to childhood.

As I have observed it, "surrender" for a child is a commitment of his life to God, made while he is young, and before a radical turn-about is necessary in order to bring the life in line with God's will. It means that the clay is molded in its true form before it has become set. There is great hope in that. It is a perfectly normal thing for a child to want to let God, whom he loves and whom he knows loves him, have the ruling direction in his life. If this experience is grounded in honest living, it is sound and growing.

We emphasize the necessity for the daily time of prayer and listening to God's guidance as of extreme importance for continuance in the Christian life. In the class we always start the lesson period with a time of prayerful listening, usually not longer than three to five minutes for the small children and eight minutes for the older boys and girls. The children catch the naturalness of it very quickly and enter in enthusiastically. No pressure is exerted to make them pray aloud or even to share their guidance with the others. The teacher must set the example of honest and simple sharing, and even a shy child cannot long resist the atmosphere of honest confidence.

It is more of a problem to persuade the child to have a daily quiet time at home, especially in homes where there is little coöperation from the parents. But once the child has grasped the idea that it is through listening to God every day that he will know God's will for that day, an effort will be made to observe this time regularly. A little notebook in which to write down guidance is an added incentive. In a class of older girls four-fifths of them keep a daily quiet time with considerable regularity.

The final test is, of course, in the living out of the experience. The teacher must have vision for the pupils to keep pace with their growth. The best gift is one of so building the experience of God upon a moral foundation and a thorough acquaintance with the faith of Bible characters and of Jesus Christ himself and his revelation of God, that the child literally roots his life in God.

2. A Teacher of Young Children[1]

The teacher who wrote the following statement is now Director of Religious Education in a southern city of the United States. The material was originally broadcast over the radio from one of the large stations in New York City.

The modern trend in education today is toward life centered courses. We aim to teach our children those things which will aid their all-round development from day to day, from year to year. We try to inculcate right habits of self-control. We want them to make the proper adjustments to their ever changing environment, physical, social and intellectual.

We are learning more and more each day how best to do these things which we feel are a necessary part of the child's education. Psychology has helped us a great deal, with its emphasis on the laws of learning and habit formation; with its constant stressing of the importance of the individual and his need of careful guidance.

The schools have been alert to all these new phases of the educative process and have turned them to good

[1] The writer is Miss Sarah Elizabeth Gustam, for two years a teacher of lower grades in Calvary Church School, later, Director of Religious Education in Church of the Holy Comforter, Burlington, N. C.

use. Our children learn Arithmetic, Spelling, Geography, History and all the other subjects that now enrich the curriculum, according to carefully worked out psychological formulae. School subjects are graded according to the age and need of the child. Even the number of minutes given to each subject has been determined so that the child may obtain the maximum results from his efforts to learn.

Knowing these things and understanding their value to your child, you would not think of sending him to any but the best modern school, where the teachers are trained in the newest educational practice, and where your child's problems will be adequately met.

But with all this new knowledge and with all the modern emphasis on habit formation and character-training, our children are not receiving all that they need to fit them for life. Often schools are unable to give them a knowledge of God or a belief in prayer. In the education of our children, spiritual training is a necessity at every step. Yet, we who insist upon our children being taught in the most modern way and who would shudder at the thought of ever going back to the old inefficient mass method of teaching, are content to do little or nothing about their religious education. We may get the children ready on Sunday morning and march them off to Sunday school, where, during a period of time varying from fifteen minutes to a half-hour, we expect them to get a knowledge of religion that will stay with them throughout their lives.

I remember an instance that happened once when Holy Thursday and the chief fast day of the Passover came on the same date and in a city where the day was not a school holiday. Children of Roman Catholic, Episcopalian, and Jewish families were permitted to go home; in fact, many of them did not even present themselves in school. Children of other denominations were indignant at the discrimination shown in the gift of what to them was a holiday and wanted to know why. The teacher told them she would ask the absentees next day. Not one of the excused children could give a correct answer. The fact that not one out of the fifty children questioned, all of whom had asked to be excused from school for the religious holiday, could tell why it *was* a holiday is proof that one half-hour a week is not adequate to teach all the facts of our religion.

Then, too, in religious education, as well as in academic, we need to build up right habits, attitudes, and appreciations. We want our children to be honest, truthful, unselfish. These things are learned and become habits through attentive repetition followed by satisfaction. We want our children to have a sense of spiritual values. These are not born in the child. All that the child brings to his study of religion is a great faith. He believes what he is told by those whom he has learned to trust, his parents and his teacher. At first he is docile and accepts without question the fact of God and the power of prayer. But then comes a time of transition. The child comes into contact with the larger world outside. He observes the way people act, he listens to what they say, and he wonders about it all.

This country was brought into being by people who believed in the power of family prayer. Now we are too busy to take time to gather together and pray to God for direction and blessing. We do remind the children, especially when they are small, to say their prayers. But there is such a difference between saying your prayers and praying. The first becomes mechanical, but the second is a constant path to God. Surround the child with the atmosphere of prayer and he will pray. We want our children to have a sense of spiritual values. How can this be achieved more effectively than through that kind of prayer that convicts and shows the way. It is our duty to give to our children the habit of prayer that is spontaneous, natural, and continuous. This is built up like any other habit, by constant repetition, growing satisfaction, and joy in communing with God. This will be facilitated if the parents in the home will take their share of the responsibility. If the power of prayer is visible in *our* lives the child will make the right reaction.

The sister of a friend of mine found this to be true. Her problem was what to do with her four-year-old daughter when she said, "I won't." Both had strong wills and fiery tempers. When Dorothy refused to drink her glass of ovaltine at bedtime, her mother lost her temper and tried to force obedience. This was as effective as force usually is, and the results might have been disastrous had not the mother remembered, in the midst of her anger, that both were children of God. She turned to her little girl and said, quietly, "Let us ask our Heavenly Father what we should do about this." Together they prayed. When their prayer was finished the mother apologized to Dorothy for being irritable and getting angry. Dorothy, too, had an apology to make and then she jumped into bed. A minute later she was out again and drank the ovaltine without a word.

These are not isolated cases. Parents and children are really finding the solution to their disciplinary problems in the fellowship of prayer. This is done by children and adults meeting on an equal basis in the presence of God, who understands before we tell Him and longs to have us come to Him for the solution of our problems.

Prayer should begin when the child is old enough to take the attitude of prayer, whether or not he understands. It should be a constantly growing experience of God. The child should learn to share his plans, his ambitions, his griefs, and his joys, to ask for light and to look to God for help and direction. This growing concept of God will be strengthened in the child if he hears stories of others who have experienced the power of God in their lives. The grand old Bible stories of Abraham and Isaac, Joseph and Moses, Saint Paul and Timothy, all have a message of God's love and power to guide, that the child should know. From infancy he should hear the stories of Jesus, how he lived as a boy and as a man, and what he taught. As the child grows older he should learn to apply those teachings to his own life.

Because it is impossible to teach in a half-hour a week all these things that the child should possess if he is to know God when he is grown, there should be classes for week-day religious education, for all children, where they can learn to know and to love the stories of the Bible and to find a real relationship with God through prayer. This week-day religious education is important. Our children need it if they are to be trained to be active and intelligent Christians. But these classes can only be effective if they are working hand in hand with the parents. The influence and responsibility of parents are greater than any school instruction. Encourage your child in his search for God. Go with him and help him because if he learns to love and serve God now, naturally and joyously, when he is grown he will not depart from the Way.

CHAPTER XII

THE USE OF THE STORY

How curious it is that so many of us forget our own childhood and all the children we know, and become immediately terrifyingly serious and grown-up when we think of religious education or when we attempt to teach children to know God and to know the Bible! Most curious of all is it that we forget the value of the story, and that in spite of the quantity of literature that has been written about telling stories to children, we turn to preachments, to enforcing moral lessons, to credal doctrines, and other things the minds of both children and youth will reject when driven in upon them before they are ready to understand them, or worse still, when they could grasp them through their own self-activity if given a chance.

We know that the day-school teacher relies upon the story for first impressions, for illustration, for development of an idea. We know that the good teacher leaves to the child's own initiative and self-expression the statement of the moral, if there be one, or of the truth or fact the story aims to teach, standing by, meanwhile, to say the correcting or guiding word when one is needed to prevent error, often using a repetition of the story itself, in slightly altered form, to guide the child into right thinking, rather than direct counsel or assertion. Why are we so slow to apply the valuable method thus learned and commended to our religious instruction?

Or possibly I should rather say to our teaching of the Bible. For in many of our church schools, the story method is in use, but in many the stories are not Bible stories and when the Bible itself is taught the story method is not used. In too many of them the stories told are of the "goody-goody" sort, compared to their great disadvantage by the children with the stories of their day-school experience, generally sceptically regarded, often leading to secret resolutions not to be a "muff" or a "gump" or a "tame guy" or some other term of the day or school for some one who is too good to be true. We have stopped feeding "Elsie" books to our girls, or "Sanford and Merton" to our boys, as their reading material, a serious deprivation, I believe, for such literature has in the past unconsciously fostered high ideals of conduct. Yet at the same time that censors of child literature have rejected such stories in the general reading of youth, religious stories for children retain the same style. The comparison is inevitably made and religion suffers. I have had a score of books in my hand lately, all relying on such stories to carry over essential and desirable religious truths, some of the stories without any literary value, patently made up to point a moral, incidents outside of the children's possible range of experience. One really great book as an aid to teachers is spoiled by its use of this type of story. Such stories are an outrage upon children's intelligence. When I read them or hear them, I often want to tell the story-teller, "The devil is using you to disgust children with religion."

My earnest plea is that teachers and parents use the Bible stories, the stories of the early Christians, stories of the saints, of the struggles of the Christian church in successive phases of its existence. It is *religion* you are teaching. Go to its source.

Our difficulty is that we have gone so far away from its source that we do not know its stories to tell. The time has come for us to learn them over again for ourselves and freshen our own religious thinking thereby. There is no moral truth, there is no desirable trait of character to be imitated, there is no error the evil consequences of which need to be pointed out, which may not be shown to children by means of a Bible story. Find them. Learn them. Re-state them in the language of the day, even into the "lingo" or even "slang" of the children's daily speech. And tell them again and again. Learn how to tell them.

MAKING A BIBLE STORY EFFECTIVE

Have you ever heard a banquet speaker mangle a good story? Have you ever laughed in spite of yourself at a story you have already heard scores of times? Of course you have done both. Did you ever apply such experiences to your own telling of a Bible story, whether to children or to a congregation or in illustration of a principle of Christian living you wanted to make clear and concrete? If not, it is time you did, for Bible stories can be found to illustrate and to emphasize every problem in life and they should receive carefully practiced telling. Also they are quite apt to be new to a fairly large part of your audience in these recent, Bible-neglected days, and you can be sure of a "hit" if you learn how to tell your story well.

Every quality needed to make a banquet story effective is essential in telling Bible stories, and while what I am about to say is intended to guide parents and teachers in telling Bible stories to children, I have found it of use in public speaking where Bible stories served to point a moral.

Some preliminary suggestions may prevent your falling into some common errors about Bible story-telling. Don't formalize the telling of Bible stories. The story of Shadrach, Meshach, and Abednego or of Joseph and his brothers can be made as thrillingly interesting as the story of Epaminondas so dear to children's hearts today, and there is no reason whatever for making the wonderful Old Testament stories just named any more stilted or old-fashioned in language than the other. Nor should Bible stories be formalized by being confined to any one period of a day or to periods of religious instruction. I knew a family of children to whom the story of the three boys in the burning fiery furnace was the favorite bedtime story years before they knew it came from the Bible. And don't everlastingly label every story as a Bible story!

Next, omit details of an extremely unpleasant nature or at least don't emphasize them in a way to do harm to the mind of an unduly imaginative child. Don't take this injunction too literally or interpret it from an adult viewpoint. Stories of killing seldom horrify children. The slaughter of the Egyptians in the Red Sea will convey no more horror than the orgies of Jack the Giant-killer, unless you go into gruesome details of suffering. The story of the Crucifixion can be made a thing of great meaning for children or it can be made a long-lasting torture of the mind by dwelling upon the piercing of Jesus' side by the spear before children are old enough to understand.

Another general suggestion relates to the introduction of the Bible story. Seldom can you jump right into the story, especially if you are telling it to a group of children. They must quiet down, get into a receptive mood, be prepared to give attention without distracting or divergent interruptions. Don't delude yourself with the idea that you can begin with "Children, I'm going to tell you a Bible story," and get a row of charmed hearers at once eagerly ready to listen to you. They will almost always have something of much greater interest (to them then) to tell you as the hearer. Did you ever try to tell your story of an operation in a group of six or seven other operatees?

Remember that experience and let children use up a little surplus energy by telling you in the first two or three minutes some story of the day's incidents or of an animal some one has seen. It won't take long, for each one will soon weary of the other's story and be ready to listen when you say: "Here's a story of long, long ago," or, "I know a queer old story something like that," or some other attention-commanding remark which seems at once to make your story more attractive than any story some one of them is struggling to tell.

These general suggestions understood, we are ready to consider the essential characteristics of good story-telling, especially needful in telling Bible stories if we are to keep in mind our major aim in religious instruction—to make God a real and lasting influence in children's lives. We shall consider these characteristics under five headings: (1) Preparation, (2) Telling the story, (3) Action, (4) Illustration, (5) Reproduction.

1. *Preparation.* Chauncey Depew once said he prepared and rehearsed his stories better and more often than he did the more serious content of his banquet speeches. If this were true of one of the most famous and effective story-tellers, what preparation must you and I make of stories taken from the Book of Books to teach the history of God's revelation of Himself, His law, His love, to human beings?

The preparation should include, first of all, several readings of the story by yourself long in advance of your telling it. Read it in at least one book, preferably more, of Bible stories for children. The bookshops of the different religious denominations are full of such books. Choose one of a style pleasing your own taste for your first reading. Then read it again in a book whose language grade is suitable to the children to whom you mean to tell the story. Finally, read it in the Bible itself. Do the final reading aloud so that your own ear can catch its phrases, the rhythm and the beauty of the language, and the impressiveness of incident.

Then prepare your own version. At first you may

need to write it out in order to be sure you cannot be tripped up by a faulty memory. But you will soon find that all you need is an outline giving you sequence, the high spots, phrases to be repeated in Bible words, etc. Children do not mind your using notes, even when they object to your reading a story to them. In fact, reading to children is a totally different art from telling stories to children, and the same person is not often a success at both. Children do understand your using notes, but if you become a skillful story-teller they won't notice that you have any notes. Nevertheless, the preparation of the outline is essential for you to do, whether you use it or not when you tell the story.

An important preparatory step is the selection of your illustrative material. What this includes will be discussed under the heading, "Illustration," but it must be mentioned here because it must all be selected in advance. Many a well-told story has lost its effect through hasty or ill-chosen pictures, through the lack of any illustration, or through too many pictures leading to confused and distracted attention.

2. *Telling the Story*. Use vivid words and don't fear repetition. Most children have a curious fondness for words, especially new and vivid ones. Often in asking for a story they will use certain vivid words that have somehow caught their word-sense. The children I spoke of before always asked for the story of Shadrach and his companions as the story of the "burning, fiery furnace." Gideon's army was another favorite and it was always called the story of the "men who lapped water" with an emphasis on *lapped*. Joseph was always the boy who

had a "coat of many colors." Those words were not the only part of the story they remembered, but they served to aid memory and to identify the story as well as to catch attention in the beginning.

Repetition is valuable. To begin with, it gives emphasis to the story. Also it secures the grasping of an idea or a fact by a child who may have lost it in the first statement of it. Next it gives the child a peg on which to hang a story. If your words have been chosen so that they have a musical quality and your repetition adds a certain rhythm, you have established definite aids, not only to memory, but to feeling, closely allied to the religious emotion.

Use as many of the actual Bible words as you can without formalizing the story or interfering with children's easy understanding of the content. The words described as vivid in the instances already cited are the actual Bible words. The parables of Christ are full of words and phrases which instance this point and are possible of use even with very young children: "First the blade, then the ear, then the full corn in the ear." "Pearl of great price." "Weeping and gnashing of teeth." "He that hath ears to hear, let him hear." The entire parable of the wise and foolish builders, of the wise and foolish virgins, of the ten talents.

But besides their vividness, there is another reason for using Bible words, and that is the resultant familiarity with the Bible. The Bible cannot then become unknown country through which we may not go without a guide. When we open its covers we find a familiar friend, as we come upon these words made known through the story-telling of our childhood or youth. I feel truly sorry for the loss sustained by the hundreds of young people I meet today whose childhood had no such familiarizing with Bible stories and Biblical phraseology. It is a real literary loss as well as a spiritual and religious difficulty. How can we follow God when we know not His guide-book?

Try to tell your story straight ahead, but don't be alarmed or turned aside by children's interruptions, providing those interruptions relate to the story or lead to its interpretation or to enlargement upon it. The children won't lose the thread of the story unless you do, and a natural opportunity for repetition is provided. If there are numerous irrelevant interruptions or if the thread of the story is lost, you have erred somewhere in your preparation to tell the story. Possibly you gauged the length of the story wrongly. It may be too long. It may be monotonous. It may lack a clear recognition of the high spots. It may lack action or illustration.

3. *Action.* Action is really a part of the telling of the story, but it is so important that I list it as a separate characteristic. Use plenty of action in telling a story. Be dramatic in a truly artistic way. Use gesture in a properly controlled and appropriate manner. When you tell of the handwriting on the wall at the feast of Belshazzar, get up and in gesture write on the wall. Make the words, "Weighed in the balance and found wanting," seem to flash out on the wall.

Use the dramatic instinct of the children themselves. Let them "play-act" the stories you tell them. I went into a room at Christmas time and found teacher and class telling and acting the story of the Three Wise Men. The chairs were the camels, the curate's desk was the manger, the teacher was Mary—everything was utilized, but invested in imagination with new forms and colors that had all the effect of reality. I have never known anything more reverently done than the Christmas pageant of our church school last year. Even the adults in the congregation felt the marvel of the Bethlehem story as little actors told it in silent dramatization.

Select stories for the action that is in them, especially with little children. Remember that children learn first words and phrases that express action, long before they learn or use words that qualify nouns or verbs. Even with adults, unless you have time for reiteration and explanation, it is better to get your idea over by means of a dramatic story than to depend on description or argument.

4. *Illustration.* Make your story graphic. If you are telling the story of David and Goliath, show the valley of Elah on a map, the mountain on which the Philistines stood, and the one on the other side where Israel was. On a blackboard draw tents (triangles will do) to show the two armies arranged against each other. Have a picture of a giant and one of a young shepherd boy. Rapidly sketch (crude work will do as well as the most artistic), the helmet and the coat of mail. Have a sling and "five smooth stones." Use each, or show it as you come to the appropriate place in the story. Finish up with some one of the many pictures of David and

Goliath, copies readily obtainable at any shop supplying church-school materials.

If you are telling the story of Ruth and Naomi, show both Moab and Judah on a map. Trace the journey to Bethlehem. Show a picture of a barley-field. Make drawings to show a field in harvest and in famine time. Show a copy of the well-known picture of Ruth and Naomi, with Orpah returning to her people.

So far as possible, use pictures in color. Have as many actual objects as will fittingly illustrate your material without themselves becoming the center of interest instead of the story content. Use illustration particularly in review, in summing up, or in repetition, even more than in the original telling where you may want the emphasis to rest on the words and the action rather than on some unimportant detail of a picture.

5. *Reproduction.* In some way the story should be told back to you. Children love to tell stories as well as to hear them. Encourage them to tell the story you have just told to some younger children or to one another. Let older children write the story in their own words. Pageant and dramatization provide marvelous means of reproduction.

In addition to reproduction in words, spoken or written, and in action, induce reproduction by means of pencil, paint, or tools. Carving in soap told the whole story of Joshua and the walls of Jericho. Bits of muslin, a tiny doll, some string, and a shoe-box became the reproduction of the story of the man sick with the palsy and let down through the roof to Jesus. Huge blobs of blue crayon meant the sea, some black ones meant a boat, some lines meant the sails, and a few figures meant the disciples in the boat pleading with Jesus in the storm. Some pipe stems and some crêpe paper became the people spreading palms in front of Jesus, represented by a figure on an animal quickly cut out of wood. If anachronisms (like the American flag on the end of the boat where the disciples stood pleading!) or crudities (like the colt for Palm Sunday which was more strangely made than any animal known!)—if these occur, never mind. It is the *story* you want impressed on their minds, its lesson, its truth, its teaching of God, not an artistic creation.

Reproduction of their Bible stories and their comments become for children an easy introduction to the principle of sharing which the quiet time is to develop. If the reproduction is written, some method of preservation should be found so that eventually the child will have constructed his own book of Bible stories.

Finally, do not try to enforce a moral or an ethical or even a religious lesson with every story you tell. Let children make their own deductions—they always will. They expect you to preach at them and so they are all ready to turn a deaf ear. But the impulse, the curiosity, to know what the story means, is there and they will find it out, which is self-activity and self-expression, if we did but know those principles of teaching instead of talking about them.

A list of Bible stories I have personally found useful follows. They are also great favorites among children. They are given chronologically according to the Bible. Special favorites are listed first, then others which can and should be used to round out the children's instruction in the Bible:

CHILDREN'S FAVORITE BIBLE STORIES

Noah and the ark
Joseph and his brethren at the pit
Moses in the bulrushes
The child Samuel
David and Goliath
Solomon's decision about the babe's mother
Belshazzar's feast
Daniel and the lions' den
The burning fiery furnace
The Babe in the manger
The wise men
Calming the sea
Lord's Supper
Ananias and Sapphira
Saul on the way to Damascus
The wise and foolish builders
The good Samaritan
The lost sheep
The prodigal son

OTHER RECOMMENDED BIBLE STORIES

Lot's wife
Sacrifice of Isaac
Joseph and Benjamin and the cup
The passing through the Red Sea

Moses on Mount Sinai
The walls of Jericho and their fall
Gideon's army
Ruth and Naomi
David and Jonathan
Solomon and the Queen of Sheba
Elisha, the children, and the bears
Esther
Jesus in the temple
Healing of the nobleman's son
Feeding the 5,000
Healing of the blind man
Man sick with the palsy
Palm Sunday
Gethsemane
The betrayal
The walk to Emmaus
Stoning of Stephen
Lydia
Timothy
The mustard seed
The soils
The two debtors
The lost coin
The great feast
The wise and foolish virgins
The talents

CHAPTER XIII

MEMORIZING BIBLE VERSES

IT IS important to remember that the power to memorize anything is at its height in childhood and that it decreases rapidly after thirty is past, except when one's work has kept the power fully exercised and constantly in practice, as, for instance, in the work of the theater. It is necessary, therefore, to store one's mind in youth with the beautiful things of literature and with Bible verses, beautiful as anything in literature, inspiring to high ideals of character, comforting to call to mind in sorrow. The credit of the superior work of the English schools in language and in composition is often laid to the amount of Bible study required, as compared with the lack of it as a requirement in our schools. If no other end were desired than the enrichment of vocabulary and of poetic phrasing, the memorizing of Bible verses should be included in every curriculum. Indeed, it should begin long before a child enters a school. Hence, what is said on this subject applies to parents as well as teachers, to adults as well as children.

But there are other ends to be attained. The Bible is the source-book of inspiration to Christian living, the food by which the religious life is kept nurtured and alive, the solution for our problems in faith as well as in action. Imagine trying to solve algebraic problems without understanding the symbols or memorizing the rules of the equation! Yet in our day, thousands of young people are being started out in the life-long problem of righteous living with no knowledge of the Source-book and no memorizing of the rules God set down for problem-solving in the Book of Books. Facts of American history have recently been challenged and a great controversy set going between the so-called "debunking" historian and the extremely nationalistic patriot. To find out the truth, the reason for our faith, do we seek either one for justification of our belief or for honest, unprejudiced facts? Never, unless one wants to be deluded or to become a cynic. We turn to source-books, to original documents, to records, to reports written by scientific students of research. Why, then, seek evidence for the truth of Christian living without reference to the Great Source-book?

There is still another end to be reached, and that is the constant incitement to progress in right living and the incessant uneasiness of conscience produced by departure from Bible-teachings. Verses memorized in childhood recur accusingly to one's mind when sinful acts are committed or contemplated, and, on the other hand, bring contentment and courage when temptation has been strong and right action difficult. Even in adult life I have seen the memorizing of Bible verses operate to develop Christian living. In Calvary Mission, Mr. Hadley requires the men to memorize and recite Bible verses, a new one every week. I have seen those men incorporate the verses so learned into their daily thinking, their daily speech, and set themselves to live up to the standards inculcated. If men weakened by drink and embittered by their failures can so apply themselves and learn to reorganize their lives, why not you and I? More important still, why wait for manhood or risk failure for our children? Why not begin when their power to memorize is at its height and store their minds as full of Bible maxims and truths as of folklore?

To teach the memorizing of Bible verses is as much an art as to teach anything else. There is a right and a wrong method, whether you are memorizing for your own use or teaching some one else to learn a Bible verse, *by heart*, as we say. Let us illustrate with the Beatitudes which our church-school children have recently learned.

First of all, some "Don'ts." 1. Don't tell the student to learn even one by heart alone until after you have finished your group study of it—the group being you and he, or you and several students.

2. Don't tell him even to read it through alone. Do that *first* reading yourself aloud, so that he gets at once a right impression, right phrasing, right emphasis.

3. Don't let him read or say it aloud until, by repetition, you are reasonably sure he will read it correctly. This applies even to yourself as a lone student.

4. Don't waste too much time on explanation of meaning. Tell or, better, draw from the students, just enough to give interest and to prevent meaningless repetition. *Remember*, your aim is memorizing, not exposition. Don't be worried because the children do not fully understand. Comprehension will come to them when

they recall the words in years to come, when the power
to memorize will have faded. We do not demand that
the thirteen-year-old shall explain to us the ethics and
philosophy, or even the imagery, of "The Chambered
Nautilus," before he learns it as a memory gem in
school. Yet it is no simpler in language or in ethics
than the Beatitudes and many another Bible gem.

Let us illustrate by some suggestions about how to
proceed with the memorizing of the Beatitudes. First,
make sure that every child has a printed copy to look
at—the Bible, the Prayer Book, a Testament, or a
small Gospel of St. Matthew. Tell him to find the
fifth chapter of St. Matthew or the page in the Prayer
Book. Let him see and say, "Fifth chapter of St. Matthew." Get him to tell you that it is the first book in
the New Testament, that the Beatitudes are in the fifth
chapter. Never mind whether he can read very well or
not. You are helping him to learn to find his way in
the Bible.

Then tell him that the same word begins nine verses,
and ask him to find it. Let him say it nine times, putting his finger on each one of the nine *Blesseds* separately. Tell him that blessed is another way of saying
beatitude, that these nine verses are called the Beatitudes because each one begins with the word, blessed.
Then review a bit with questions: In what book of the
Bible do we find the Beatitudes? In what chapter of St.
Matthew do we find the Beatitudes? How many Beatitudes are there? With what word does each Beatitude
begin? Why are these nine verses called Beatitudes?
Note the repetition of the word, Beatitude. If required

of the student in his answer to each question, you will have fixed the name firmly in his memory and put behind you a name which might otherwise be a stumbling-block.

Now, read aloud to him the first two verses of the fifth chapter, he himself looking at the printed words. Then say, "I'm going to read this again while you listen or look at the book to find out where Jesus went." The answer given, "up into a mountain," read it again while he discovers why Jesus went up into a mountain. A third time to find out who came to him; a fourth time, what did Jesus do for his disciples. Thus you will have achieved four readings and familiarized him with the author of the Beatitudes and the circumstances under which they were said.

This is all preliminary, the preparation, the mind-set, as the pedagogues call it. Now you are ready to teach that first Beatitude: "Blessed are the poor in spirit; for theirs is the kingdom of heaven."

Read it aloud as the child looks at his book. Read it aloud again very slowly, emphasizing *poor in spirit*. Again, emphasizing *kingdom of heaven*. Ask him to find out, as you read it aloud for the third time, who are called *blessed* in this first Beatitude. Pause a moment for an explanation of *poor in spirit*, but do not be too exacting. Then say: "Let us now learn together who are called *blessed* in this first Beatitude," read aloud from "Blessed" through "Spirit." Question: Who are blessed? What word did Jesus say about the poor in spirit? Then for the first time, let him himself read aloud, "Blessed are the poor in spirit."

Now tell him that in every Beatitude, Jesus says *who* is blessed in the first half, and then in the second half of the Beatitude he tells *what* the blessing will be. Repeat this in slightly changed words, emphasizing who and what. Tell him to look at his book and read aloud who is blessed in the first Beatitude—"Blessed are the poor in spirit." Note that by ear and eye the child will have had ten repetitions of the first half of this first Beatitude, and no pounding of his breast as he idly and by rote repeats meaningless words!

When you are sure he has a fairly certain knowledge of the first half of this first Beatitude (the "Who is blessed?") begin work with the second half (the "What is the blessing?").

Read aloud: "For theirs is the kingdom of heaven," as he looks at the printed copy. Question just a bit on the word "kingdom." Speak of England and King George, Belgium and King Albert, Holland and Queen Wilhelmina. Bring out or tell that kingdom is where the king lives and rules. Don't try to be exact in either dictionary or political definitions. You are seeking the memorizing of a Bible verse with a fair understanding of its meaning, not a theological discussion.

Read it again as he looks at his book. Question: "What kingdom is promised to him?" "Who lives and rules in that kingdom?" "Read it yourself, very solemnly, for God is promising a share in His kingdom." "How can you share in God's kingdom?" This last question will provoke a variety of responses and will provide an opportunity to check error and remove wrong impressions. One child said once, "When God goes to hell!"

Imagine the problem for the teacher resultant from this answer given to a listening group of nearly a hundred! Don't ever laugh! If you do, repression results, and you will have hard work to get sincere and frank replies again.

Now begin again with the same or similar questions. But—this time require him to say the entire phrase, emphasizing differently each time, to show the word which carries the answer: *Kingdom, heaven, theirs.* Three more readings, three appeals to ear and eye, three learnings by repetition, result, done willingly, without force or loss of interest.

The next step is to put the two portions together, so as to make a learning of the whole Beatitude. This is done best by means of:

(1) Questions to be answered, always in the words of the Bible verse itself.

(2) Play, thus associating pleasure with the task instead of difficulty.

(3) Appeal to the spirit of competition or of emulation, always generously and humorously. To illustrate:

1. "Who will get the blessing in the first Beatitude?" The child reads the first half; by this time, he will probably say it without any book. "What is the promised blessing?" The child reads the second half. "Tell me the 'who' part of this first Beatitude." "Now tell me the 'what' part." "Can you tell me the whole of the first Beatitude?" Note the unemphasized substitution of the word, *tell*, for the word, *read*, brings about in the child the substitution of *memorized* repeating for *reading*.

2. "You say the 'who' part and I'll say the 'what' part." "Ah! I caught you! I did not look at the book!" Or change about, "You caught me." Look at the book yourself. He is spurred to greater exercise of his memory by feeling that he knows it better than you do. No answer should be accepted unless it is actually in the words of the Bible. If there are several children learning at once, separate them into groups. Let one group say the first half in answer to your question; the other group, the second half. Reverse sides. Use other questions in a similar way.

3. Gradually, but not too obviously, during the drilling by play, introduce competition and emulation. Use such devices as "I can say the whole Beatitude. Let me see if you can." "I said it all the way through without looking at the book. Can you?" "You said it all without the book. I wonder if I can." "Watch me to see if I make a mistake." Note every lip in the room will move with yours! "I'm going to listen to the girls, and then to the boys, and decide who knows it better." "Now the boys say it. Girls watch them and see if every boy knows it." Reverse this. Don't take any answer. It is not knowing which one says it better that is your aim, but repetition, learning a task, pleasurably.

Finally, associate reverence with the words learned, introducing the idea in some such way as this: "I wonder if we all know the whole Beatitude. Let us say it together." "Who said these words?" "To whom?" "We are his disciples, too. Let us say this Beatitude as if we were listening to Jesus say them as he did to the disciples." "Let us now bow our heads and say them like a prayer." "Let us look up high, as if we could see the kingdom of heaven, and say this first Beatitude to tell Jesus we want to earn that blessing." "Let us kneel and say this first Beatitude as our last prayer today, silently and reverently."

A period of twenty minutes will be needed for teaching the material so far presented. If the time allowed for memory work is limited, as it usually is, then two periods of ten minutes each will be needed. The second Beatitude can be taught in ten minutes, since the preliminary work required in detail for the first Beatitude will demand only a few questions of review.

To illustrate: "Let us say together the Beatitude we learned in our previous lesson." "Why do we call it a Beatitude?" "Who said the Beatitudes?" "To whom?" "Where was Jesus when he said the Beatitudes?" "In what book of the Bible do we find the Beatitudes?" "What chapter?" "Old or New Testament?" "What word does each Beatitude begin with?"

If the children use their books to find the answers to these questions, never mind. You are not testing memory or conducting an examination. You are trying to prepare them for the learning of the second Beatitude by refreshing their memory of the first. Do not insist upon individual answers in this review when conducted with a group, especially in a large number of children of mixed ages and grades. Fear and self-consciousness are produced, time is wasted, the attention of the majority is lost, and an unreceptive, even irritated attitude brings a wrong association with the whole lesson. Those who do not remember hear the answers of those who do remember, and your review purpose is served just as well as if you had tested out individual pupils.

Now we are ready to learn the second Beatitude— "Blessed are they that mourn; for they shall be comforted."

Read it aloud, looking at the book yourself. Make sure that the child has found the right place and is following the words with his eyes as you read. Read it aloud again, very slowly, emphasizing *they that mourn*. Again, emphasizing *shall be comforted*. Read it aloud the third time, asking him to find the "who" part of this Beatitude. Remind him that we learned in the previous lesson that every Beatitude tells *who is* blessed in the first half and *what* the blessing is in the second half.

Pause now for explanation of the word *mourn*. This will present no difficulty, as *poor in spirit* does in the first Beatitude, and it will prove helpful in teaching the other Beatitudes to have fairly exact meanings, when they can be obtained without using too much time or digression. Then say: "Let us now learn together *who* are called *blessed* in this second Beatitude." Read aloud, "Blessed are they that mourn." Question: "Who are *blessed?*" "What word did Jesus use about *they that mourn?*" Then ask the child to read aloud for himself, "Blessed are they that mourn."

Note: By this time the child will have received an *ear* impression of this first half of the second Beatitude at least eight times, also an *eye* impression if he has followed his book. This is now emphasized by speech, his own voice, as he answers the last question just given.

Make sure that this first half of the second Beatitude is learned before you proceed. Ask, requiring the complete answer each time: "What is the *who* part of the second Beatitude?" "What did Jesus say about those who mourn?" "To whom is the blessing promised in this second Beatitude?" The child will now have repeated aloud five times the words of the *who* part of the second Beatitude, and you can feel sure that he is ready to learn the second half, the "What is the blessing?"

Read it aloud, "For they shall be comforted," as he looks at his printed copy. Question a bit on the word *comforted*. Compare with a mother comforting a child who has fallen, a friend sending a letter to some one who has lost his mother, friends sympathizing with some one who has had a great disappointment. Read it again as he looks at his book. Question: "What does God promise those who mourn?" "Read it yourself, very solemnly, for you are reading God's promise which you may need sometime." "How can God comfort you?" Make a brief pause here for the variety of responses you will receive. Here is a wonderful opportunity for you to develop the idea of a spiritual experience, of the Inner Voice and its reality. But be content with the idea, the thought, the faith in the experience. Don't try to secure a definition or accurate terminology. Wait for that until the youth himself *seeks* it.

After a brief two or three minutes spent in how God comforts, begin again with the question: "What did Jesus promise those who mourn?" "Read the *what is the blessing* half of the second Beatitude." Now we are ready to put the two portions together, for it is the whole Beatitude we want the child to know. The method is the same as for teaching the first Beatitude, already suggested in this chapter and repetition is unnecessary here.

At the close, in addition to the association of reverence, as described in the close of the lesson on the first Beatitude, the second Beatitude offers an excellent opportunity for teaching intercession as a part of prayer.

Before kneeling to say the second Beatitude as a prayer, present to the child the name of some one he knows is in trouble or ask him to name some one. Then say: "Let us kneel and ask God that —— will know this promise Jesus made, and let us say this second Beatitude as a prayer for ——, "Blessed are they that mourn: for they shall be comforted."

The third, fourth, fifth, sixth, and seventh Beatitudes can be taught in the same manner and will present little difficulty or delay. The eighth and ninth are harder and will require more time. The best way is to precede each of these two with Bible stories which illustrate the *who* part of the Beatitude. For the eighth, the story of the stoning of Stephen is an excellent illustration. For the ninth—the *who* part being the eleventh verse and the *what* part being the twelfth verse—incidents in the life of Paul and quotations from his own writings afford remarkable illustration and even human evidence of the truth and faith expressed in this ninth Beatitude.

The method here given at length for teaching the Beatitudes is possible of modification and extension for teaching to children any Bible selection, whether it be an entire selection to be learned as a "memory gem" or verses to be learned in connection with a set lesson in the curriculum. In closing this chapter, however, I want to repeat most earnestly the warnings given in the four "Don'ts" at the beginning, else your child will look upon his Bible verses as a hated task and get neither beauty of language and thought nor inspiration to righteous living.

With considerable hesitation, and only because the request is so frequently made, I add a list of Bible selections it seems to me that every child should learn. Probably each reader will find some favorite of his own omitted, in which event, if there be good reason for his choice, let him add to my list.

The Beatitudes—Matthew 5:1-12.

The Ten Commandments—Exodus 20:1-17.

The Love Chapter—I Corinthians 13.

Psalms—1, 19, 23, 24, 46, 91, 100, 103, 121.

Proverbs—1:10; 3:13-18; 9:10; 12:22; 15:1; 16:3; 16:8; 16:32; 22:1; 24:19, 20; 25:11; 25:21, 22; 27:1, 2; 28:1; 31:10-31.

Prophets—Isaiah 35, 40, 53, 55.

Habakkuk 2:20.

The Gospels—Matthew 5:13-16; 6:5-15; 6:24; 7:1-5; 7:7-12.

Luke 2:8-20; 14; 15.

I Corinthians 15:58.

The Epistles—Romans 8:1; 12.
Ephesians 6.
Philippians 3:14; 4:4-13.
I Timothy 6:6-12.
Hebrews 12:12; James 1.
I John 1:5-10; 2:1-3.

CHAPTER XIV

NOTES ON CURRICULUM AND METHOD

THERE has been so much of real value written on these two questions, curriculum and method, that any lengthy discussion is not needed. I wish there were space to give a list of books I have found helpful in my own work. I would urge every church-school teacher and every parent to begin a library of reference books on religious education selected according to the several needs and circumstances. At the same time, I would express two warnings:

1. It is difficult to find in print an entirely satisfactory curriculum for church schools or course of Bible study for parents to use with children at home. In 1928 I consulted most of those then existing and I have read several new ones since. Some are very good, some are miserably poor. Many have two mistakes in common. They are written by adults from the adult point of view of what children should know, and are resultantly foreign to childhood and to modern youth. And they are graded according to the grades of academic education in public or private schools, ignoring the fact that the material to be read or studied, being for information, should have no language obstacles and should therefore be at least one grade simpler in language and style than the child's listed academic grade.

Therefore, any printed curriculum you use must be supplemented by additional reading by the children and by aids to the teacher, and it must be adapted to the conditions of your individual church school.

2. It is unwise to follow slavishly any books on religious education. Read them, digest what you read, select and use what God guides you to see as true, reject the rest. One of the most helpful books I ever read on religious education contained a vast amount of material I had to reject because the author evidently doubted our Christian view of the life of Christ, and I was very careful about putting it into the hands of young teachers. There is another serious danger in following exactly any printed curriculum or methodology —that is, the discouragement to the teacher's initiative and the lack of incentive to careful preparation.

The best illustration of what I mean about how to select and adapt a curriculum or a method of religious education must come out of experience. In our church school we had three serious considerations to keep in mind, as revealed to us in the early conferences.

1. We are a downtown church. Therefore we have a migratory population. Furthermore, the children come from two extremes of the social scale. These facts precipitated, five years ago, a number of questions. Should there be some scheme of separation of these two extremes, involving, as they did, not only differences in social background, but also in race and nationality? The children, we knew, would present no objection to a democratic solution, but would the wealthier, more cultured parents permit their children to remain in the

school? Yet how could we, either as Christians or as Americans, make class distinctions, especially when our number was so small that any scheme of separation would be a definite training in class distinction, snobbishness on the one side and sullen resentment on the other? How could we follow a graded course of instruction when the children migrate to and from schools with a different or differently graded course? What system of grading would we accept, that of the near-by public school? or which one of the private schools the children attended?

2. We had no trained teachers except one or two who had experience in academic schools. We had no money to employ trained teachers, and we had very real doubts as to whether it was right to hire teachers and whether teachers, so hired, would be found to have the qualities we wanted. We were too far downtown for it to be expedient for our teachers to join any training-school of religious education then in existence. We had no time to establish a training-school for ourselves and most of us were too busy to be able to continue such a training-school in the future, even if established. Several of our teachers, especially the men, were engaged in some profession or business and could not fairly be asked to meet the requirements of the training-schools, even if distance permitted.

3. We felt strongly that the life and teachings of Jesus Christ should be the basis of all our teaching and that therefore no semester should pass without the inclusion of definite instruction in the New Testament. This conviction presented several difficulties in adopting

any printed curriculum, especially when added to the fact of a migratory population.

All of these and many other issues which arose in regard to our church-school curriculum were thoroughly threshed out at teachers' meetings and at innumerable quiet times of special groups. There was no committee or director appointed to study and decide on solutions, the teachers and children then accepting results with unthinking, or at best unchallenging, obedience. Some statement of how we met some of these issues may be suggestive to others similarly placed, although this book offers neither a curriculum nor a textbook on method.

First, our united guidance was that our third consideration must be in our curriculum, every semester, even if other work were sacrificed. We met this in our first year by spending the entire time on the study of the life and teachings of Christ. We divided the material, not by Gospels, but by subject and time of the year, and arranged so that the birth, youth, and early ministry climaxed at Christmas; the Last Week at Easter time; selected parables during Lent; his teachings including particularly Matthew 5, 6, and 7 and John 14, 15, during other times of the year; all being gathered together in a chronological review in the late spring.

In succeeding years we interrupted our chosen curriculum at Advent for the story of the birth, youth, and certain selected teachings desirable for memorizing; and at Lent for the study of Christ's third year of ministry, ending at Easter as in the first year.

Second, after some experimentation, we agreed not

to use a curriculum in which each grade had a different subject of study. Instead we agreed to use the same subject of study for the entire school, but to grade the material in quantity, language, approach, and illustration. Roughly indicated, this meant in our first year that our youngest children learned the Christmas story; the intermediate grades learned the entire story of all the events in the first thirty years of Christ's life, given historically and including all four Gospels; the highest grades and the Bible classes covered all of the same material plus a comparison of the four Gospels, Old Testament references, and some traditional stories. All in the same period of time. A similar procedure was followed in each subsequent division of the work that year.

In each succeeding year we have used the same plan of grading, whatever the curriculum used. Up to date, we have never used any printed curriculum in its entirety, and we put no printed book, except the Bible itself, into the hands of any pupil. We are deeply indebted for suggestion and direction to many sources, especially the curriculum plans published by the National Council of the Protestant Episcopal Church and by the Sunday School Board of the Presbyterian Church in the United States.

We do not say that this is finally conclusive. We do say that in a situation like ours, with special conditions to meet, our plan has worked and teachers and children are interested and happy.

Third, our problem of class distinctions settled itself most amusingly and has never arisen since as a real issue. The children really settled it in two incidents which I cannot refrain from relating, using fictitious names for the children involved.

The first incident occurred at our first church-school party, parents and children invited. One child is the grandchild of wealthy people and connected with a number of people of high social standing. She was then three or four years old and had begun to attend our kindergarten. Some relatives who believed in our aims brought her to the kindergarten and were considerably disturbed to find that we kept the entire group together, black and white, Armenian and Mayflower descent, tenement and Park Avenue dwellers. But Susie adored it all and insisted that her aristocratic relative bring her to the party.

The other child, Florence, is black. Her father is caretaker in a big apartment house on the Park. He and his wife are intelligent people and were for years communicants in an Episcopal church in a district entirely composed of colored people. When they came downtown to our district, where there are no colored people, even though many of the white people are poorer and less well-bred than themselves, they faced the question of religious education for their children and discussed it with one of our teachers. We took the two children into our school. It was for this child, Florence, that the cherished Susie conceived a strong liking, which fact was unknown to teachers or family until the day of the church-school party.

Susie arrived late, in care of a handsomely dressed and impressive relative, who paused at the door in order to select seats without disturbing the exercises. But

Susie's quick eyes discovered a vacant seat next to her beloved Florence, and, breaking away, she ran up the aisle to greet Florence so affectionately that we all saw it. The relative's only comment to me later was, "And so that's that!"

The other incident involved three boys the following summer. One boy was Jimmie, Florence's brother, a wiry little colored boy, very clever at games. One was Billy, who came from a family and home similar to Susie's. The third was Tom, who represented a different element altogether. His people are honest and respectable, but they are very poor and live in a tenement house in a neighborhood none too good. Tom reflects his environment rather than his parents. A teacher who was a silent observer of the scene which occurred among the three boys told me the story.

Several games had been played, in all of which Jimmie had excelled. Then Tom began to bully Jimmie and finally shouted at him: "You get out of here. We won't have any niggers in our games." But Billy, the aristocrat, squared up to Tom and said:

"Oh yes, we will. The only thing that's the matter with you is that he plays a better game than you do."

One most important problem in church-school organization we can just barely mention. That is worship and the worship service. To be absolutely honest, we do not feel that we have yet arrived at a finally satisfactory answer as to worship, although we do know that we have eliminated many of the regrettable circumstances which so often accompany a worship service in a church school, especially among boys. We have secured reverence and attention, and that without discipline or preaching. The plan in use during this past year is the best yet evolved, but the chaplain, Mr. Cuyler, the assistant superintendent, Miss Parmelee, and Mrs. Bell, the choir mother, are seeking for a plan which will make the worship service as real and spiritual in character and influence as the class-room quiet times.

And they are right, for worship is the maximum expression of our devotion and consecration to God and of our purpose to live as He guides and as He has revealed His will to us. When we can impart to our children such thought of worship, we need not fear their temporary departure into curious human interpretations of life's alpha and omega. When our thought of worship is right, we do not permit it to become a mechanical, dull thing associated with a particular place at a particular time. Instead, worship becomes a part of our morning arising; of our walks in woods and gardens so that we see God in every leaf and flower; of our errands in city streets so that we see His hopes for man in the individuals who pass us by; above all, a part of every ideal, of every contact, which shapes our life-experience. Thus we see a reason for service, life becomes Christ-centered, and we can say with Paul, "For the love of Christ constraineth us."

THE END

OTHER BOOKS BY TUCHY PALMIERI

Books That Are Currently Published,
With A Short Overview Of Each

INSPIRATIONAL/MOTIVATIONAL BOOKS

TUCHY'S LAW AND OTHER CONTRARIAN QUOTES TO HELP YOU IN LIFE'S JOURNEY

A life-affirming and thought-provoking collection of quips, quotes, and proverbs that were gathered and honed by the author and his family, friends, and colleagues over a twenty-five-year period. Covering topics as diverse as ambition, success, initiative, and handling setbacks, the more than one thousand warm and witty sayings in this book will bring a smile to your face and leave you nodding in recognition.

THE PLATINUM RULE AND OTHER CONTRARIAN SAYINGS: THE FIRST 60 YEARS

This is a collection of contrarian quotes. For example, W.C. Fields' contrarian quote was, "If at first you do not succeed, try again. Then give up and don't make a fool of yourself."

Another quote is The Platinum Rule: "Do unto others as they would have you do unto them." The

<u>Platinum Rule and Other Contrarian Sayings</u> is a warm, witty, and life-affirming collection of quips, quotes, and aphorisms that will touch your heart and bring a smile to your face. Gathered and honed by the author over a forty-year period, the 522 sayings in this book will bring back fond memories on the topics of family, work, self-worth, dealing with adversity, aging gracefully, and many, many more.

JOSEPHINE, IN HER WORDS: OUR MOM

A collection of words of wisdom and related comments that Mom had given us over the last sixty years. It was a 90th birthday gift to Mom. The reviews on Mom's book started what I refer to as interactive books/workbooks. In essence it was a method of enabling the reader to record any thoughts, desires, and memories that came about while reading the quotes and words of wisdom.

PHIL, IN HIS WORDS: OUR DAD

An interactive book that enables the reader to write down words of wisdom from his/her dad that were triggered as the wisdom words of my dad were read. An excellent way to bring back a deceased parent. Dad had been gone fifteen years when this book was created. The source of the book was from several people who knew Dad. As an experiment we took the grandchildren and the great-grandchildren who were too young to remember Dad, and read highlights of the book to them. The result was phenomenal. Dad was transformed from being just a picture on the wall to a real person who had passed down ways of being to their moms, dads, and grandparents.

The words and wisdom of a devoted father, collected and recorded by a loving son, <u>Phil, In His Words: Our Dad</u> will resonate with adult children of all ages and backgrounds who remember and appreciate the gifts given to them by their parents. So often it is the wisdom of our fathers, grandfathers, mothers, and grandmothers that encouraged us to take the right path in life. The reading of Phil's words may trigger the words that were given to you, the reader. You are encouraged to write them down to reflect on, to pass on to your children, and to share with friends. You are encouraged to write down your favorite words to pass on to future generations. Enjoy Phil's words and may they help you in some way.

<u>SEX AND INTIMACY: THE GIFTS OF LIFE</u>

A serious and yet light-hearted book of tactics, techniques and tools to make relationships work better. It approaches sex and intimacy with great words of wisdom from people in all walks of life. Many words brought humor and lightness to this hard and hot topic. The words in <u>Sex and Intimacy: The Gifts of Life</u> are given by wise men, famous people, and common folks and are intended to give the reader truisms, advice, and comfort in the areas of sex and intimacy. It is our belief that sex and intimacy are God-given gifts to be enjoyed as any other gift. We also believe that the healthier people's sex lives are, the happier and healthier people are in all aspects of life. Recent research verifies the benefits of having sex on a regular basis. Sex can be fun, exciting, and a great way to become closer with your partner. Sex can also be great for your health, since your sexual health and mental well-being are closely linked. You are encouraged to use this interactive book to jot down and record ideas which, when implemented, would make your sex life healthier and happier.

MONEY AND SO MUCH MORE: THE TRUE MEANING OF WEALTH

A book filled with wisdom from the famous and not-so-famous from ancient times and from current times. Again the goal of the book is to inspire people to put money in its right place, not have it rule them, and how to be wise with money.

Money and So Much More: The True Meaning of Wealth is designed to shift a person's relationship to money so that it no longer brings upset and worry. This is achieved by using quotes, proverbs, famous sayings, anonymous words, and humor. In addition, the book is interactive, and the reader is encouraged to put into writing his or her thoughts and actions as they relate to money. Through these words the reader is moved to be different in the world and that money will take its appropriate place in life, thus allowing one to be free of money's grip.

OPRAH, IN HER WORDS: OUR AMERICAN PRINCESS

Many of Oprah Winfrey's wise words are enhanced by the addition of suggested affirmations, inquiries, and suggested action. The goal of the book is to make Oprah's words personal to the reader by giving suggestions and allowing interactivity through writing in the book in the appropriate space. Oprah, In Her Words: Our American Princess, is filled with quotes from Oprah Winfrey expanded to include suggested affirmations, inquiries, and actions. Readers are given space in which to create or to take on their own affirmations, inquiries, and actions. The book is divided into challenging topics with words designed to inspire, encourage, and assist.

OBAMA, IN HIS OWN WORDS: PRE-ELECTION

Filled with the quotes, speeches, and words that Barack Obama used that helped him win the election. The goal of the book is to go beyond the pictures and create a historical keepsake of his words. This dynamic, interactive workbook shares with the reader the words Barack Obama gave us before and during his campaign; words that moved, inspired, and touched many of us. They collectively propelled him into the White House as the 44th President of the United States. May this collection of words serve as the beginning of the Obama legacy. He comes to the presidency with one of the highest approval ratings of our modern presidents. May he serve us well. God bless America, and God bless you.

SATISFYING SUCCESS: AND THE WAYS TO ACHIEVE IT

This book helps the reader to find the rare space of creating success that satisfies rather than success that is empty. Success is one of the strangest phenomena in life. First, it is often subjective, and it has been elusive for many as it is often not well defined. Many who work their whole lives finally achieve it, only to find that it is a hollow victory, void of any satisfaction. In this inspiring and thought-provoking book one can discover the paths to satisfying success. You are encouraged to take from the words of others those that resonate for you and leave the ones that do not. You can indeed have both success and satisfaction at the same time. This book proves that it can be done and has been done for others.

RELATIONSHIP MAGIC

Relationship Magic is both a reference book and an interactive workbook. The book is based on the belief that relationships are alive and, like everything that lives, require nourishment. Inside the book the reader will find nourishing words of wisdom, wit, and humor from both the wise and the famous and also from everyday people. In addition, the book offers the reader places to write down their own wants, needs, and desires for a relationship.

RECOVERY BOOKS

OFF THE WALL CONTRARIAN QUOTES FOR PEOPLE IN RECOVERY

The goal of this book is to provide the person working with an alcohol problem more tips, tactics, and tools to strengthen recovery. (I am a recovering alcoholic, sobriety date April 14th, 1986.) This book is a collection of poignant, touching, and truthful thoughts and phrases related to the recovery process. Inspired by AA's 12-step program, this book provides hope and inspiration for anyone dealing with addiction and substance abuse issues. As with material presented in and around the rooms, it is suggested that you take what works and leave the rest. What does not work today may work for you tomorrow, which is why it is a good idea to pick up the book as often as you can. Program tools are a key to many people's recovery and this book gives you an opportunity to use several tools. 1) Reading recovery literature. 2) Writing–take a quote each day, write it down and carry it with you. 3) Meditation–by pondering or meditating on a quote you can improve your conscious contact with God. 4) Telephone–sharing a quote with a friend helps both. 5) Anonymity–many of the quotes and healing writings are from unknown authors. May their anonymity help you in your time of need.

THE FOOD CONTRARIAN: QUOTES FOR PEOPLE RECOVERING FROM OR DEALING WITH EATING ISSUES

A book filled with tips, tactics, and tools to help people with eating issues. It utilizes the 12 steps as a foundation and brings fresh ideas and strategies to assist the compulsive eater or non-eater. (I lost two brothers from food-related illnesses. I am also a grateful recovering compulsive overeater, in the program since March of 1991.) This book is a collection of poignant, touching, and truthful thoughts and phrases related to recovery from eating disorders or other food addictions. Inspired by AA's 12-step program, this book provides hope and inspiration for anyone dealing with food-related issues. 1) A dishonest mistake– a lie. 2) Some people do the steps by sidestepping. 3) Count your blessings instead of counting your calories. 4) DIET: Doing Insane Eating Temporarily. 5) For the anorexic too little is too much. NOT FOR STUDY PURPOSES LIGHT READING WITH SERIOUS PONDERING Suggestion: Read one or two per day, write them down on a piece of paper and post or carry with you. 1) Relapse: When your disease is in recovery. 2) Binge: When enough is not enough. 3) Purge: An attempt to correct a mistake with another mistake. 4) Bulimia: Two wrongs to make right.

RELATIONSHIP RECOVERY: HEALING ONE RELATIONSHIP AT A TIME

This book is all-encompassing and is suggested for anyone working a 12-step program of any kind as it is most likely that the problem has its roots in relationship to a greater or lesser degree. <u>Relationship Recovery</u> is about using the 12-step program principles to help anyone suffering from relationship ills. While not approved by any 12-step program, it is a great addition to the literature offered to help in doing the steps, especially steps 3 through 12. Resolving relationship issues is the foundational key to any 12-step program, and recovery cannot occur without addressing it. This workbook is intended to help people in that endeavor.

REPUBLISHED CLASSIC GEMS

<u>WHEN MAN LISTENS</u> by Cecil Rose

Cecil Rose was very rare. A book of how to listen to God. In his preface, Cecil Rose writes, "The chapters of this book are an attempt to set down briefly the simple elements of Christian living. I believe that there is nothing in them which cannot be found in the New Testament." What Cecil Rose wrote was a model for living that went beyond the Christian faith. It became one of the sources of the 12-step recovery program, which has brought many people to God. It embodies universal principles that serves all of mankind. It is an excellent guide for people of the Christian faith; people who are struggling with their 12-step program; people seeking to deepen their spiritual/religious connection; people who are seeking to live a life of honor and integrity in a world filled with the opposite. It is my honor and pleasure to have Cecil Rose's work reborn through this reprinting so that the masses can have access to his words and the principles he speaks of.

TWICE BORN MEN: A CLINIC OF REGENERATION
by Harold Begbie

A famous English author of the early 1900s writes stories of downtrodden people who were saved by the works of the Salvation Army, a movement that started in England and has spread to 116 countries today.

THE GENIUS OF FELLOWSHIP/THE CONVERSION OF THE CHURCH by Sam Shoemaker

Sam Shoemaker, the man who started it all, was a pioneer in both the Oxford movement and A.A. He presents in his book The Conversion of the Church how the church needs to operate like a fellowship and that in reality the fellowship is the church. Sam mentions in his foreword that the original church was often called the fellowship. A.A. is often referred to as "The Fellowship." Sam devotes an entire chapter to the genius of fellowship. There he emphasizes the importance of fellowship in the church: "When the Church is alive the desire for fellowship is alive." Sam gives his definition of real fellowship: "The core and genius of real fellowship as I see it, is the power to live and work with people upon the basis of absolute love and honesty."

CHILDREN OF THE SECOND BIRTH: WHAT WE USED TO BE LIKE, WHAT HAPPENED, AND WHAT WE ARE LIKE NOW by Sam Shoemaker

The movement that helped Bill W. to recover. An early Sam Shoemaker book originally published in the 1920s, Children of the Second Birth is filled with stories of men and women who had their lives changed by turning to God; stories of people who, under the guidance of Sam, utilized the Oxford Group principles and found miracles. These men and women came from the depths of desperation and despair to places of happiness and joy. The touching journeys that they went through gave others the hope that they too could have a new life filled with peace and serenity. People today can achieve the same results as the people mentioned in this book. All that is required is to follow what they did. May these true-life accounts help you or your loved ones find the happiness of God.

TWICE BORN MINISTERS: WE ARE ALL MINISTERS
by Samuel M. Shoemaker

Twice-Born Ministers is a book of twelve personal stories of twelve ministers who were reborn and re-energized to do the real work of ministry by helping people to become faithful followers in every sense of the word, specifically being reborn themselves to Christ and to his calling for them to do his work.

LIFE CHANGERS: 13th EDITION by Harold Begbie

Frank Buchman: the man who started the Oxford Movement. Life Changers is comprised of century-old stories of men who had their lives changed so profoundly and so dramatically that the original book was reprinted 12 times. Now 100 years later, with its 13th printing, this precious classic is set to change the lives of many more men and women. The words in this book are as true today as they were then.

<u>Life Changers</u> is also about a man, Frank Buchman, who was first and foremost a teacher. Buchman could change the lives of students and scholars in the course of a single conversation; changing those lives so profoundly and persuasively that the world was in disbelief. Buchman started a movement that reached the shores of America and lives today in the form of many 12-step programs. While the original movement was founded on Christianity, its principles and ideas moved beyond religion and Christianity into a more generic spiritual movement.

FICTION

<u>THE GODSONS: THE TRINITY ALLIANCE</u> by Carl Palmieri and Don Gerrard

Tracing 37 years in the life of one powerful Sicilian-American organized crime family, <u>The Godsons</u> is a story that cries out to be heard. A decade in the making and based on years of painstaking research and historically-documented accounts, this novel gives the reader insight into the greatest power shift in the history of our nation; a shift that has affected virtually every state in the union. While many of the characters in the book are fictional, much of the story is based on real events that have occurred, and continue to occur, in our country and around the world every day. Appealing to readers interested in learning more about the secretive inner-workings of the U.S. government, The Godsons exposes the corruption of government at all levels and explains how, through one unholy alliance, a single family is able to tear down centuries of laws and traditions and dominate U.S. policy to the White House and beyond.

ABOUT THE AUTHOR

Carl "Tuchy" Palmieri was born in 1942 in an old mansion belonging to the former mill owner of the factory where his father worked. His family was one of six related families that occupied the mansion. The second son of Italian immigrants, Carl grew up in Westport, Connecticut. After receiving a bachelor's degree in business administration from the University of Bridgeport he began his career marketing and installing accounting computers for the Burroughs Corporation. Twenty-one years later, in 1987, he started his own computer business. Carl is also the author of a series of self-help books.

Today Carl lives with his wife, Susan, in Fairfield, Connecticut. He has three children, two stepchildren, and 13 grandchildren. His nickname, Tuchy, comes from having been one of three Carls in his family. There was a "Big Carl," a "Carl the Twin," and "Carluch," which meant "Little Carl." "Carluch" evolved into "Carlatuch," "Tuch," and finally, "Tuchy."

Made in the USA
Columbia, SC
29 July 2021